New

D1454334

GODODDIN
The Earliest British Literature

Gododdin

THE EARLIEST BRITISH LITERATURE

Gwyn Thomas

Gomer

Published by Gomer Press,
Llandysul, Ceredigion, SA44 4JL

ISBN 978-1-84851-573-4

A CIP record for this title is available from
the British Library.

Printed and bound in Wales at
Gomer Press, Llandysul, Ceredigion.

CONTENTS

Sir Ifor Williams 7

Map 8

Introduction 9

Abbreviations *&c* 34

Gododdin 35

The Gorchanau 128

A Select Bibliography 142

About the Author 144

EARLY BRITAIN – PRYDAIN FORE

PRYDYN

Bannawg
Alltglud

Merin Iuddew

MANAW

STRAD
CLUD

Din Eidyn

Lindisfarne

GODODDIN

Aeron

BERNICIA
(BRYNAICH)

Kintyre

RHEGED

Idon

ERECHWYDD

Merin Rheged

LLWYFENYDD

Catraeth

MANAW

DEIRA
(DEIFR)

ELFED

GWYNEDD

MERCIA

POWYS

Introduction

IN 1896, the Welsh manuscript called *Llyfr Aneirin,* The Book of Aneirin, or *Gododdin* (which will be used from now on, with or without the definite article), was bought for the Cardiff Free Library after previously being kept in various places in Wales. It remained at Cardiff until it was transferred to the National Library of Wales in 2010. Some have called the language of this manuscript 'Cumbric': this term denotes the 'Welsh' that was, at one time, spoken in the north of Britain. It is a geographical tag and does not refer to a language that was different from Welsh. The latest palaeographical scrutiny of the manuscript dates it to the second half of the thirteenth century. It was written by two Hands, Hand A and Hand B as they are called. One or two palaeographers have detected a third hand, Hand C, in the manuscript, but Daniel Huws, the foremost authority on the Book of Aneirin, has said that Hand C '[can] be quietly laid to rest'. Experts have ascribed pages 1.1 to 23.5 and 25.1 to 30.11 to Hand A; and pages 23.6 to 24.21 and 30.12 to 38.22 to Hand B. Hand B's text is later than that of hand A; how much later is not known. Although text B is later than text A, it is more archaic, as it is written in an earlier orthography than A. The manuscript is not complete in its present form; some leaves have been torn out.

The main content of the manuscript is a series or collection of *awdlau,* or odes – Welsh odes, as defined below. It is a collection of poems but has, at times, been wrongly called one poem. Most of the odes of the *Gododdin*, but not all of them (cf. Odes 2 and 3) are short, rhymed poems, that commemorate a planned attack by a retinue of probably 300 *élite* British warriors '*er prynu breithell Gatraeth*' (Ode 32: 'to redeem [or win back] the land of Catraeth'), Catraeth being the modern Catterick on the Swale, near Richmond. It is unlikely that this troop of warriors went out on a marauding expedition, because the year's preparation, mentioned in the poetry, suggests something more purposeful than random raids, and it is said that an attack on Catraeth was '*neges Mynyddawg*' (Ode 66A: 'Mynyddawg's mission or campaign'). The attack occurred towards the end of the sixth century.

In some of the odes (probably of later composition), the number of warriors is 363, a more 'elegant' number – consisting of a 3; 2 × 3 = 6; and another 3 – for people obsessed with threes and triads. These select warriors were gathered together in Din Eidyn, the modern Edinburgh, in the then British and Welsh-speaking kingdom of the Gododdin tribe, by a leader traditionally called Mynyddawg Mwynfawr – Mynyddawg of Great Wealth. The name of this leader has been questioned – could not the leader have been Gwlyged or Gwlgawd with his court at Mynyddawg Mwynfawr? But it makes better sense to me to think of him as a man rather than, literally, 'mountainous great-wealth', or even 'a luxurious mountain court', and his name as a leader is part of a long tradition. In the *Gododdin*, Gwlyged or Gwlgawd is mentioned as the person in charge of the feasting at Din Eidyn.

In *Trioedd Ynys Prydein – The Welsh Triads*, edited by Rachel Bromwich, which are a kind of medieval directory to traditional Welsh lore, the retinue of Eidyn, in Catraeth, is named as the retinue of Mynyddawg. The warriors came from the Gododdin itself and from other, mainly British, kingdoms. In the odes, the word 'Gododdin' is used for the kingdom in *yr Hen Ogledd*, the Old North, as the region is called in Welsh, that is, southern Scotland and northern England. In the poetry, it is also used for the British tribe living in this kingdom, and for the collection of odes attributed to Aneirin. The warriors probably slept in *pebyllau* (tents) and, by day, trained for combat. In the evenings they feasted and drank in the hall of Eidyn, with what consequences for their combat fitness we are not told. This went on for a year. Then this select retinue of warrior-horsemen travelled south and came face to face with an Anglian army of thousands – according to the *Gododdin* – from Bernicia and Deira, the modern Northumbria, somewhere in the vicinity of Catterick. These 300 Britons faced thousands. If one finds that hard to swallow, consider the 300 Spartans who faced – according to some historians – 5,000,000 Persians at the small pass of Thermopylae. However heroic a troop of warriors may be, it seems to us contrary to common sense that the men of Gododdin should have gone out to do battle against such a massive enemy force and, if that actually happened, then surely it was 'a serious strategic mistake' as Jenny Rowland put it.

What the *Gododdin* tells us, with proud repetition, is that the encounter of the Britons with the Angles ended in the defeat of the Britons, but that this defeat was glorious and heroic. In some odes it is said that there was only one survivor, others state there were three, or four. About 80 of the warriors are named in the odes; we say 'about' because some words may or may not be personal names. Whether all of the 300 were named at one time, we cannot know, and the manuscript does not contain 300 odes. Does this mean that many odes have been lost, or does it mean that a few core odes related to the battle have grown in number? Is the text reductive or accumulative? The most probable answer is that it is 'accumulative'.

The text that we have contains some *Gododdin* poems that are not connected with the raid on Catraeth, and then there are some other poems that do not belong to the Gododdin kingdom at all. But someone, or more than one, thought that all the poems in the text are the *Gododdin* of Aneirin. This became a traditionally held belief for some centuries in northern Britain, and is a belief that persisted in Wales for several centuries. The tradition became part of the 'story' of the Welsh.

So we have a thirteenth-century text that purports to tell the story of an attack that happened in the late sixth century. Is there any external evidence that the poetry of the Book of Aneirin belongs to an earlier period than the thirteenth century? Yes. Firstly, there is a poem by Owain Cyfeiliog, called *Hirlas Owain*, the long blue drinking-horn of Owain, composed about an attack by Owain's men to liberate his brother Meurig in 1155. It is located in Owain's court, and he calls on the cup-bearer to hand the 'hirlas' to each man of the retinue in turn. This reminds him of the heroic host that attacked Catraeth:

> *Ciglau am dâl medd myned haid – Gatraeth*
> *Cywir eu harfaeth, arfau lliwaid.*
> *Cosgordd Fynyddawg, am eu cysgaid*
> *Cawsant eu hadrawdd, casflawdd fleiniaid.*

> I heard of a payment of mead made for the going of the retinue, of loyal intent, with coloured [or, more probably, *llifaid* 'sharpened'] weapons to Catraeth. The retinue of Mynyddawg: for their sleep [of death] they have been talked of – enemy-frighteners, front-fighters.

It should be noted that Owain Cyfeiliog assumes that the host was the host of Mynyddawg, and not that of Gwlyged.

Therefore, in the middle of the twelfth century the story, or the 'history' of the retinue that attacked in Catraeth was known in Wales. Aneirin and his poems are also named in one thirteenth-century poem by Dafydd Benfras (*fl.* 1230–60): he refers to singing praise like 'Aneirin, / The day he sang the *Gododdin*'.

In the tale of *Culhwch and Olwen*, the text of which is found in fourteenth-century manuscripts, but whose date of composition in its final form is dated by both Rachel Bromwich and D. Simon Evans to around 1100, and whose first redaction is tentatively dated *c*.1000 by John T. Koch, there are ridiculous lists of proper names, and a few of the persons named occur in the *Gododdin*. The most notable among them is *Gwlgawd* (or *Gwlyged*) *Gododdin*, who had a horn of plenty – which is what one would expect of a man in charge of a feast. These names pre-date the Book of Aneirin.

In another poem 'In Praise of Cadwallon' – Cadwallon being a king of Gwynedd, in north Wales, who died in 633 – the line:

eilywed Gatraeth fawr fygedawg
the sorrow / destruction of Catraeth, great and famous

occurs. This line is not quite the no-nonsense evidence provided by the *Hirlas Owain*, but it does indicate that in the first half of the seventh century some catastrophe that had occurred in Catraeth was remembered in Wales. Unfortunately, before we can dash off our QED about Catraeth on the basis of this poem, we have to bear in mind that the earliest surviving copy of it belongs to the seventeenth century, although it must also be added that it contains linguistic forms that belong to a much earlier period.

But the most reassuring – Dark Ages' reassuring – reference to Aneirin, the author of the *Gododdin*, occurs in a manuscript copy of the *Historia Brittonum* (History of the Britons) attributed to Nennius, a Welsh monk. This work belongs to the beginning of the ninth century, but probably derives from an earlier source which could be as early as *c*.700. In a section of the *Historia* dealing with the wars of the Britons and Angles, there is a reference to Ida, son of Eobba, in an English genealogy. After this section come the words here translated:

Then Dutigirn [R. Outigirn > Eudeyrn] at that time used to fight bravely against the nation of the Angles. Then Talhaern Tataguen [Talhaearn Tad Awen > Talhaearn Father of the Muse] gained renown in poetry; and Neirin [Aneirin] and Taliesin and Bluchbard [Blwchfardd] and Cian, who is called Gueinth Guaut [> Gwenith Gwawd = the Wheat of Song] gained renown at the same time in British poetry.

Since Ida reigned in Northumbria from 547 to 559 we have a record of a Neirin (Aneirin), who was known as a poet in the second half of the sixth century.

It is a pity that Aneirin did not sit down and write his own poetry; that would have saved a great deal of bother. He didn't, and what we have is a late text of his *Gododdin*. What do the orthography and grammar of the text in the manuscript we have of the *Gododdin* by Hand A and Hand B reveal, and how can we say that Hand B is more archaic than Hand A? The Welsh language evolved from the British or Brittonic branch of the P-Celtic language during the period *c.*AD 450 to 600. By now linguistic definitions are more refined than the pattern of development presented in this thesis: to be precise I should, perhaps, refer to a definition such as Archaic Neo-Brittonic and so on, but the pattern chosen will serve my purpose. The Welsh of the period between the end of the sixth century and the later eighth century is called Primitive Welsh; the period of Old Welsh extends from the late eighth century – or probably earlier – to about the middle of the twelfth; the period of Middle Welsh extends from the twelfth century to about the fourteenth century; and the period of Modern Welsh follows from then on. If the *Gododdin* belongs to the latter half of the sixth century, should not the language of the text be Primitive Welsh? Yes. We can ask another question: would Welsh have evolved sufficiently by the late sixth century for Aneirin to have composed the *Gododdin* in this new language? Answer: why not?

Several linguistic changes occurred during the evolution from Brittonic to Middle Welsh. One of them was the development of lenition. In modern Welsh lenition, or mutation, is the term used for initial consonant changes in words: lenition is now a grammatical feature of Welsh (e.g. an initial *b* may become *f*). But early lenition began as phonetic changes, not grammatical changes. Another major change that occurred was the loss of final syllables of Brittonic words. These two major linguistic changes can be exemplified in a very simple way by considering what happened to one word, *abona,* the Brittonic word for *river.*

The consonant *b* between the two vowels, *a* and *o,* changed to *f (v)* > *afona*: this is an example of lenition. That's one major change.

The accent was so emphatically on the penultimate syllable of *abóna* that the final syllable, *a,* disappeared – the declensional ending was lost – giving us the Modern Welsh word *afon.* And that's the second major change.

But after the loss of the old final syllable, the stress or emphasis was on the new final syllable of the word, *afón.* These changes occurred between the middle of the fifth century and the end of the sixth: that is, Brittonic evolved into Welsh.

In Middle Welsh and Modern Welsh the stress in almost all words, that are not monosyllabic, is on the penultimate syllable: *áfon.* So in the new language, Welsh, another accent shift occurred, the stress moved from the last syllable to the penultimate: the general opinion is that this happened in the eleventh century, or maybe earlier. This is another major linguistic change.

It would be neat and tidy if we were able to set forth the features of Primitive Welsh and compare them with Aneirin's text. Unfortunately, examples of Primitive Welsh are confined to inscriptions and a few names in Latin texts, which makes comparison impossible. But John T. Koch has produced – by means of very erudite linguistic deduction and reconstruction – a text of the *Gododdin* restored to a 'more original state', in what he calls Archaic Neo-Brittonic. This is, as Ifor Williams had referred to the prospect of such an exercise, a 'new creation'. Koch has accurately described deducing a primitive core as the result of a search for material that lies 'submerged within a matrix of wholesale linguistic modernisation, textual corruption, and literary accretion, the accumulated result of centuries of oral and written transmission'.

We have already said that the B text of the *Gododdin* is more archaic than the A text. How do we know? Because its orthography is more like that of Old Welsh, for which there are records, than Middle Welsh. At one time it was assumed that this put back the date of the text to the ninth century but, as we have seen, the orthography of Old Welsh lasted until about the middle of the twelfth century. Let us take one line as an example, from Ode 66 Hand A and 66 Hand B:

> *ar neges mynydawc mynawc maon* (66A)
> On the campaign of Mynyddawg, lord of hosts

> *ar les minidauc marchauc maon* (66B)
> For the good of Mynyddawg, horseman of hosts

The orthography of the words *minidauc* (*Mynyddawg*) and *marchauc* (*marchawg*: horseman, knight) is older than that of *mynydawc* and *mynawc*. The older orthography suggests that the *Gododdin*, or parts of it, were in existence in the period of Old Welsh, from as early as the ninth century to as late as the twelfth. This takes us somewhat nearer the time of the action recounted in the *Gododdin*. John T. Koch has argued that some of the corruptions disfiguring the surviving text can be based on an earlier orthography, and he has suggested, in detail, which poems may be archaic and which may not. Anyone interested in a detailed examination of the linguistic features of the *Gododdin* should consult his edition of the text. Patrick Sims-Williams has suggested that *faulty* memorisation, but not necessarily oral transmission from reciter to reciter, almost certainly explains some of the variations between the A and B texts of the *Gododdin*.

Recent intense examinations of early texts by linguists and historians have revealed hidden matters, and given rise to some contrary speculations; this is bound to be the nature of things when the topic discussed happens to be in the Dark Ages. If we attempt to summarise the state of play, without too many caveats, we can say:

§ that the certainty in the *Gododdin* about the enemy at Catraeth being the warriors of Deira and Bernicia, plain and simple, may not necessarily be so;

§ that historians and archaeologists are involved in attempting to determine whether the *Gododdin*, or some part of it, can belong to the late sixth century or not;

§ that concerning the matter of the migration of the text to Wales, questions have been raised about whether the moving text or texts were oral or written. Did an oral *Gododdin* tradition pass from Lleuddiniawn (Lothian) to Strad Clud (Strathclyde) before the seventh century? Did the basis of the A text pass from Strathclyde to Wales, also in the seventh century, while the B text remained in Strathclyde for another two centuries? Or was it, as Koch proposes, more likely that there was written transmission, from the seventh century, rather than centuries of purely oral transmission?

These considerations are important because the *Gododdin* may well be the oldest British literature – British, rather than Welsh, because it precedes any literature in any of the other languages of Britain. Kenneth Jackson, no doubt with a twinkle in his eye, provocatively called his English edition of the *Gododdin*, 'the oldest Scottish poem' which, to any ardent Welsh person – highly literate as we are – is as appropriate as calling Joyce's Irish novel *Ulysses* an Italo-Franco-Swiss composition. A. O. H. Jarman's response, as I take it, was to call his edition 'Britain's Oldest Heroic Poem'. This has created a kind of contest where the constant element is the earliness of the text, a contest in which I found myself obliged to take part, hence the 'Earliest British Literature' of the title. It means that this Welsh poetry is the earliest composition in any of the languages of Britain.

From a historical aspect, it is unfortunate that we do not have any other pleasantly straight historical account, or any other evidence that corroborates the *Gododdin*'s version of the battle at Catraeth. But we do know that by 638 Din Eidyn had been occupied by the Angles. So something had happened.

Some discussion of the historical details of the *Gododdin*, which may have a bearing on its historical authenticity, has concentrated on the method of warfare that is described in it. This matter is mentioned here because it is an important feature of this war poetry. For example, the kind of historical considerations that have been raised are:

Did the warriors fight on horseback? Did they ride to the battlefield on horses and then dismount in order to fight? Was there an army on foot accompanying them?

The text states, in no uncertain terms, that the British warriors fought on horseback – maybe following the example of Roman cavalry. They rode horses that were smaller than modern horses, but horses that were, nevertheless, big enough to be called *cadfeirch* (war-horses). It would hardly be heroic for a warrior to ride to battle on a Shetland pony. Whether one can throw a javelin or spear effectively from the back of a horse without stirrups has been an issue. That, of course, would depend on who is riding the horse. We should remember that the warriors in the *Gododdin* did have enough time to practise performing the sort of *campau* (feats) that can certainly be performed by adept horse-riders. Compare the feats of the Gododdin horsemen with the feats of some present-day Mongolian riders. One thing that is very clear in the *Gododdin* is that the poet and his society set great store by their steeds, and that horses were symbols of high status.

The weapons that the warriors fought with were swords and spears, which could be used to throw and to thrust. They had shields and mail-coats to defend themselves. Details of warfare are repeated throughout the odes.

In recent years, the study of oral literature has become a minor industry, and detailed discussions of living oral literature and the search for signs of orality in written literature have pro-liferated. Although theories about early written versions of the *Gododdin* have been persuasively presented, the fact still remains that between the late sixth century and the Book of Aneirin not one line of the text survives. In fact, only small fragments of Welsh verse, such as the *englynion* in the Juvencus manuscript, in Cambridge University Library, survive to indicate that Welsh poetry was being written down by the late ninth or early tenth centuries.

Let's consider what could have happened to a text in a period of oral literature in Wales. It would have been a period when it was one of the tasks of the professional poets, or possibly, poem-declaimers, to memorise poems, and to declaim them to some kind of accompanying beat of a lyre or harp. But it is likely that there would have been, as well as memorisation, some impro-visation, or even composition: the *gwarchanau* or *gorchanau* (see below) are clear evidence of this. Nevertheless, memorisation was important in the bardic tradition. The kind of poems that we find in the *Gododdin* belong to a very old Celtic tradition, where bards – according to Classical authors – sang the praises of the heroes killed in war, to send their souls down the ages. This concept of praise poetry continued to be a part of the bardic tradition in Wales and Ireland for centuries. In a defence of the poetic art in Ireland Giolla Brighde declared: 'Were it not for poetry, sweet-tongued harp or *tiompán* [we] would not know of a goodly hero after his death, nor of his reputation nor his prowess'. It is very likely that the poems of Aneirin would have been handed down from one generation of poets to the next. Indeed, in the Book of Aneirin there is an indication that there were competitions for memorising important poems:

> Every *awdl* [ode] of the *Gododdin* is worth one song in singing because of [its] honour in a song competition [or bardic contest]. Every one of the Gwarchanau [Songs] is worth three songs and three score and three hundred. And the reason is for keeping the memory in the Songs of the number of men who went to Catraeth. Than that a man ought to go to fight without arms, a poet ought not to go to a contention [bardic competition] without this Song [that is, the Song of Cynfelyn]. Here now begins the Song of Maeldderw. Taliesin sang it and gave honour to it. [It is worth] as much as all the *awdlau* [odes] of the *Gododdin* and its three Songs in a song competition.

This is a rather odd note, but it states that one short ode of the *Gododdin* would be worth one point in a competition, but that one of the longer 'Songs' – that is the Songs of Tudfwlch, Adebon, and Cynfelyn, all associated with the *Gododdin* – would be worth 363 points each, the number, according to some odes in the *Gododdin*, of the men who went to Catraeth. But the last 'Song', the Song of Maeldderw, is worth the sum of all the short odes of the *Gododdin*, and its three 'Songs' (3 songs × 363 = 1,089 + the number of odes). We are told that Taliesin, another of the *cynfeirdd*, or early poets, sang it, and by clear implication, that he was – in someone's opinion – far superior to Aneirin.

Points awarded for poems in the Book of Taliesin suggest that the poets may have had some system of accomplishment and assignment of points – however bizarre or improbable this point-system may appear to us. There may be a suggestion in the quirky poem 'Cad Goddau' ('The Battle of the Trees') in the Book of Taliesin that the Song of Maeldderw has magical properties.

Before the twentieth century, rural populations were, on the whole, more settled than they are now. In rural communities, many families lived in a particular part of the country for hundreds of years. They passed on a great deal of language and lore from one generation to the next, and so memories were kept alive for a long time. In Wales, industrialisation, education, the modern media, and Anglicisation eroded this long folk memory. But Welsh folk memory has lasted into the twenty-first century. It is always a pleasant surprise to realise that words, poems, sayings and customs that ought to have been swept away by now have a tenacious persistence. In the Welsh version of Ode 1 in this book the word *ethy* occurs. Even Sir Ifor Williams, the scholar who elucidated the *Gododdin*, did not know of any other example of it. He suggested that the form of the word was *eddi* and went on to suggest that it meant 'trimmings' or 'fringes'. Many years after the publication of Sir Ifor's edition I was told by a farmer from Bala, in north Wales, that *eddi* was a word he used for the long, trailing green growth, or fringes, of plants in water: the word was still in use.

In a poem to 'The Gull' by the fourteenth-century poet Dafydd ap Gwilym, one line refers to that bird as *dyrnfol heli* (sea gauntlet). A dead word? So I thought, until I heard a friend referring to the strong glove worn by those cutting thorn hedges as *dyrnwil*, a form of *dyrnfol*: the word was still in use.

My friend, the late Professor Bedwyr Lewis Jones, heard that the sharp east wind in Powys was described as *Gwynt o'r hen Bengwern* (the wind from old Pengwern): Pengwern is the name used for the region around Shrewsbury in the poetry of Llywarch Hen, which probably belongs to the ninth or tenth century. Once again, the memory of the name had persisted.

A student at home for his long summer vacation was told by a woman how fortunate he was, *Ni raid i'r dedwydd ond ei eni* ('the Fortunate need only be born'), a line which is found complete in a gnomic verse which is hundreds of years old, and which recalls an old belief that all persons are born either Fortunate (for whom all things will go well, whatever they do) or Unfortunate (for whom all things will go badly, whatever they do). If ancient matters survive in the memories of ordinary folk, we can expect a more detailed remembering but, apparently, not a perfect remembering in a poetic tradition that valued memorising. A text – or, shall we say, the nucleus of a work of literature – can be retained for centuries in oral memory, even though that text may be affected by 'wholesale linguistic modernisation, textual corruption, and literary accretion'. The fact that we have more than one version of many of the odes in the *Gododdin* gives us some idea of what happened to a text in the course of centuries, and in the course of its migration from the 'Old North' to Wales. The term 'Old North', in Wales, suggests an affinity between the British kingdoms of northern Britain and Wales, an affinity which may, or may not, have some connection with the migration to Wales of 'Cunedda with his sons' from Manaw Gododdin some time around AD 400, Manaw being a sub-region of the Gododdin, with its main centre at Stirling. We ought not to expect the dating of the earliest records of early oral material to be entirely linked to ink and parchment or even, as in our case, a defined period in the evolution of the Welsh language.

How did the *Gododdin* come to be written down? Either the poets or the declaimers who memorised and recited the text, or parts of it, wrote it down; or, more probably (as later evidence suggests that it is unlikely that the early poets could write), others memorised the odes, after a fashion, and transcribed them, or – could it be? – transcribed them from dictation. And were poems that had been written then read out aloud, as is suggested by the lines from Ode 83 that I have translated as:

> What is seen is what will
> [Later] be read out aloud.

It is unfortunate that the meaning here is rather uncertain. These transcribers, probably not just Hand A and Hand B, working at various periods were almost certainly clerics. What now remains of the *Gododdin* is what was written down by Hand A and Hand B.

Sir Ifor Williams first published his edition of the *Gododdin* (*Canu Aneirin*) in 1938. He had been brought up in a practically monoglot Welsh village, and he naturally profited from the accumulated wisdom and memories that so enriched the Welsh of the people with whom he grew up. For him, the odes of Aneirin fitted into a living context, and it shows.

The geographical setting of the *Gododdin* is most definitely the 'Old North', as we have said. The names of places, where they can be identified, are mainly names from this area – except when references are made to warriors from other British kingdoms, as for example Gwynedd; or from Pictland. The historical setting, with the Angles advancing northwards from the eastern sea-board, seems authentic, and a British effort either to do them some damage at some strategic point, like Catraeth, seems plausible.

The poems, most of them short, in the *Gododdin* are called *awdlau* (odes). Many of them are *awdlau* in the strict sense of a poem composed with one end-rhyme throughout; others have more than one end-rhyme. In addition, there are rhymes within some lines of the poetry as well. In the Middle Ages, Welsh poetry was syllabic, and there were metres in various syllabic patterns, with a specified number of syllables per line. The number of syllables in the 'patterns' of lines in the *Gododdin* is not constant, and it makes sense to think of them as lines with a number of stresses. What constitutes a 'line' of poetry in the *Gododdin* can be interpreted in more than one way. Sir Ifor Williams said that it was obvious that the early poets – including Aneirin – thought in long lines of from 12 syllables to the occasional 20 syllables, but long lines with sections to them. He printed the opening part of Ode 1 as two lines (the orthography has been modernised, and the stresses indicated are as they would be in Middle Welsh):

> /   /
> *Greddyf gŵr oed gwas*

Either 4 or 5 syllables – depending on the pronunciation of the first word as *greddf,* or *greddyf,* with 2 stresses.

> /   /
> *Gwryd am ddias*   (5 syllables, 2 stresses)
> In might, a man: the age span of a lad;
> In war, [a warrior] full of valour.

But he could have printed it as one line:

> *Greddyf gŵr oed gwas gwryd am ddias.* (9 or 10 syllables)

The American scholar Eve E. Sweetser has claimed that the basis of the metrics of early Welsh verse is based 'on a two-stress line, with a one-stress catalectic [lacking a syllable in the last foot] variant'. Short line or long line: it depends on one's conception of Aneirin's unit of thought, or on the 'audition' of his metric 'line'.

We have said that the lines of the odes are not regularly syllabic (though many lines are), and we can say that various line patterns suggest that they may be on their way to becoming some of the strict metres, the syllabic metres, of the later poetic tradition.

As we have said, all the lines or sections of an *awdl* may

rhyme, or the rhyme may change within an *awdl*. Therefore, in the orchestration of the poems, rhyme is the most prominent feature:

> *Teithi edmygant*
> *tri llwry nofant*
> *pymwnt a phymcant* (Ode 18)

> They revere lawful rights,
> They stain their three spears
> [In the blood of] five hundred and fifty.

There are also many half-rhymes in the *Gododdin*. They are of two types; one is called *proest*, where the vowels in two word endings are different but the consonants are the same: *doded*: *molud*. Ifor Williams called the other type an 'Irish rhyme'. Here, the vowels in two word endings are the same, but the consonants are different: *llafnawr* : *annawdd*.

Alliteration, or consonance, is prominent in the odes, and it may be that, at one time, it was strengthened by ignoring initial lenition – which would have been typical of the conservative nature of the poetic tradition. There is vowel resonance: *ethy eur* (gold-embroidered fringes); and consonant resonance: *medd yfynt melyn melys maglawr* (they drank mead – yellow and sweet, and ensnaring). There are lines which can be called lines of what later became *cynghanedd* (harmony, or 'chimes', made up of an orderly resonance of consonants within a line of poetry, or of internal rhyme, or of a combination of these), one of the most prominent features of the later Welsh strict-metre poetry:

> *Blwyddyn bu LLewyn LLawer / cerddawr*
> For a year many a singer was joyful

In several lines there are signs of *cynganeddion* in embryo.

All of these auditory features contribute to the rich orchestration of this Welsh poetry. Other features of this poetry are:

§ fondness for playing with the meanings of words, as in the ode to the hero called Heinif, which also means 'lively' or 'agile' – words which are used about him;

§ formulaic repetition of descriptions of heroes and their prowess;

§ a fondness for understatement;

§ exciting and striking contrasts.

In combination, all these create a dramatic and powerfully resonant impression of the action and the heroism of Catraeth. The verse has the incantatory power of ritual. It is proper for us to remember that the work of Aneirin, at the very beginning of the Welsh poetic tradition is, in fact, the continuation of an earlier Celtic tradition. The resonances in the *awdlau* are profound.

The *Gododdin* leaves us with a very positive feeling of heroism. The poet does not doubt the wisdom of the course of action taken or feel sorry for what happened at Catraeth. In this respect the *Gododdin* is very different from the saga poetry of Llywarch Hen (Llywarch the Old) and Heledd, of the ninth or tenth century: that poetry overtly embraces the 'heroic code' but the wailing lament in it, and the death wish of Llywarch, who seems to say, 'Would that I had died with my fellows when I was young, rather than live on to drag myself around in misery', undermines the heroic ethos. The warriors of Mynyddawg fulfilled their contract to their lord, they 'paid for their mead', and 'were worth their mead' – mead being the visible symbol of that contract.

It is the glory of the warrior-hero that the *Gododdin* celebrates, and the fact that they were not victorious does not, in any way, tarnish their heroism for there is also a sadness in the *awdlau*. The naming of the dead is always evocative of the life that has been lost, as all war memorials testify. Aneirin names dead heroes, some of them young men he had known, with a sad pride. That is why the most accurate impression of the *Gododdin* is Joseph Loth's *'grand poème lyrico-épique'*: the feeling of loss for the glorious dead is the 'lyrical' aspect of the poetry, and the 'epic' aspect of it – in a loose sense – is the celebration of the heroism of its warriors.

In this translation I have adopted Sir Ifor Williams' order of *awdlau*, though it does not follow the order of the manuscript. Indeed, this order has been called 'idiosyncratic', and even as a front-row admirer of Sir Ifor, I have to admit that this description is not incorrect. In an attempt to make it less idiosyncratic I have indicated clearly the number of the page where an ode appears in the manuscript, and noted whether the text is written by Hand A or B. I have followed Sir Ifor's order because this allows us to compare what appeared, to him, to be different versions of the same ode. Whether many of us would agree with him on all his 'likenesses' is debatable.

I have not followed his line numbering, and have, from time to time in the translation, split some lines in two.

I have often translated the actual words in the different versions of the 'same' *awdlau* – unless they appear not to make any sense to me – so that the differences in the versions become apparent.

Where words do not make sense to me, or others, or where they make better sense with emendations, I have indicated the emendations to the text with an 'R.' in the footnote.

Occasionally, two versions of the same *awdl* have been conflated, after an attempt has been made to translate them separately. Unless there is a particular reason for printing the text as it appears in the manuscript – as there is in any comparison of Texts A and B – I have modernised it.

In order to show what the typical differences are between two texts of what Sir Ifor Williams took to be the same basic *awdl*, let us consider a few examples. We'll begin with Ode 20A and 20B:

§ the same hero is named in both versions: in A we have *Breichiawr*, and in B, *Breichiawl* – the different consonants, *r* and *l*, at the end are not significant because this change occurs from time to time as, for example, in the Welsh word for 'February': *Chwefror, Chwefrol*;

§ the B text is longer;

§ only 3 lines match in the two versions;

§ similar ideas are expressed, but not in the same words: B has *gwas nyf* ('land of Heaven'), A has *gwaeanad* ('glory');

§ some words seem to have been misheard: B *esgynnai* (in this context, 'retreat'), A *disgynnai* ('attack'). Misheard, or maybe changed deliberately as in the following example: B *thechud* ('retreat'), A *phechud* ('sin'): *pechud* suggests a monkish emendation. Or it may have been that A did not understand the words in an earlier version.

If we compare Ode 22A and 22B, we see that:

§ both versions probably commemorate the same hero, though the form of the name is different: B has *Llif*, and A has *Llifiau*;

§ the two versions have only two lines in common;

§ A appears to have the correct form of the words *neus adraut* ('[The men of Gododdin] . . . recount'), whilst B has either misheard or misread an earlier text and has *ny sathraut* ('not trampled') – though, it should be added, that there is a hole in the manuscript between *ny* and *sathraut*, and only part of the *s* is to be seen.

Ode 87 is longer than the odes we have examined, and provides a variety of differences, which are set out below:

Hand A	Hand B
1 A difference of one or more letters, which can affect the meanings of words:	
rodawr	*rodawc*
gwythawc	*gwychauc*

28

gweith	*with*
gelwideint	*gwelydeint*
a	*ae*
ervei	*uruei* (The name of the hero's father.)
a phan	*a chan*

2 Different orthography:

gwythawc	*gwychauc*
ban ry godhet	*pan ry godet*
garw	*gwaro*
mynawc	*menavc*
ar rud	*ar grud* (Lenition may not have been indicated in B.)

3 Words which have been split differently:

yg cat	*y gat*
bedin agkysgoget	*bit en anysgoget*

4 The idea expressed is similar in A and B, but the words are different:

llavyn	*llain*
teyrn teithiawc	*brenhin teithiauc*

5 Different words on a similar basic idea:

diffreidyeit	*diffret*

6 More words in one text than the other:

cann calan a darmerthei	*gant can yg calan darmerthei*
llary hael etvynt digythrud	*hael etvynt doeth dygyrchet*

(There may be glosses in both of the last examples.)

7 Different word order:

o glot a chet echiawc	*y get ae glot ae echiauc*

8 Different words altogether:

yt vyd cat voryon	*bit get uoron*
cochro llann	*gwychyrolyon*

9   Similar ideas, but a difference in more than one word:

*yng gwyndyt gwaed **Glyt** gwaredawc*

*ud gwyndyt gwaet **Kilyd** gwaredauc*

(Note that the name of an ancestor in these lines is different in the two texts.)

*neut bed **Garthwys Hir** o dir rywonyawc*

*uot bed **Gorthyn Hir** o orthir rywynauc*

(The hero's name is different in the two lines.)

These examples show what can happen to a text that is heavily formulaic, in oral and scriptorial transmission. We should perhaps explain that, in this context, a formula is an idea expressed, many times, in more or less the same words. There may have even been floating formulae which could have become attached to one or more heroes. Some examples of typical *Gododdin* formulae and topoi – which are, again in this context, commonplace or typical descriptions – would be:

§   that the hero always fought in the most dangerous stations in battle, in the front or on the wing of an army;

§   that his shield was shattered from many battles;

§   that he died young, before he had any opportunity to be married;

§   that, at court, he would be shy before a maid, but that on the field of battle he would be completely different.

We could ask whether this last topos is an incipient and early example of what later became the ideal of *amour courtois*. Or does it indicate that some of these odes had been influenced by that ideal in a period that is certainly later than the time of the *Gododdin*. Before we sniff at the possibility of the presence of this ideal in a text as old as the *Gododdin,* it should be borne in mind that something like it occurs – early on, from the point of view of its 'Continental' beginnings – in the work of the Welsh Court Poets.

There are some poems in the manuscript that do not belong to the *Gododdin*. We have already said that not every ode in the *Gododdin* proper refers to the attack on Catraeth, but those odes are still part of the work. Other poems are – to us – additions or interpolations, and they have been marked with a star in this book. Dr Morfydd E. Owen has rightly pointed out that in the *Gododdin* text there appears to be a shadow of a Tale of Aneirin, and that references in the text to his confinement in an underground prison, and his release from there with the aid of Cenau son of Llywarch (Ode 49), may be part of such a tale. She has also suggested that the words spoken in the first person in Ode 48 could be a stray verse from a saga, maybe one like the Tale of Taliesin or Myrddin.

The long poems called *gwarchanau* (the later form is *gorchanau*) at the end of this book are very difficult, and contain many words whose meanings are not at all clear. My translation of parts of these can at best be called, and hopefully be called, informed conjecture. *Gorchan* can be translated as 'Song', but it probably meant something more than a 'song': the prefix *gor-* suggests this, as does the Irish cognate of the Welsh word. The Irish cognate *forcanim* means 'I learn'. So *gorchan* probably means a song with an instructive element, what may be called in Welsh *gwers* or lesson, or some wisdom in it. Why should it be so? The 'wisdom' and proverbs in these poems may be there because Aneirin's fame cast him as a 'wise' poet as, in much the same way, Virgil's fame cast him as a 'wizard' as well as a poet. When discussing the *gorchanau* Koch says, perceptively, that their presence 'implies a mode of preliterate transmission in which a master sings a poem and his pupil repeats or echoes him'. We can but hope that no pupil was hard of hearing: a suspicion that some of them were can sometimes make its way into the mind of the reader of the *Gododdin* text.

The *gorchanau* or songs of Tudfwlch, Cynfelyn, and

Maeldderw (claimed in the manuscript to be a poem by Taliesin, another of the early Welsh poets) do contain lines about heroism and warriors. There are some references to Eidyn, and the names of warriors mentioned in the *Gododdin* appear. The *gorchanau* seem to be poems that recall some of the men and the exploits of the Gododdin and other warriors, and may well be part of some bardic appreciation of the verse of Aneirin. The comment on the value of the *awdlau* of Aneirin and the *gorchanau* in bardic memorising competitions could well be part of keeping the memory of the great Battle of Catraeth alive. It would be typical of the professional poets to make competition more difficult by composing long poems to be memorised – they were always as keen to keep people out of their order as to keep themselves in; that is why, through the Middle Ages, they tried to make their craft more complicated, more skilled, and more difficult. With the passing of time, odds and ends were added to these *gorchanau*, so much so that the Song of Adebon has nothing at all to do with the *Gododdin*: it is a collection of sayings and proverbs and gnomic wisdom. Such material also found its way into the Song of Maeldderw. The Song of Cynfelyn contains interpolations, as if one or more persons were trying to define to himself, or themselves, what the basic material was all about. It may well be that the drinking of mead – large amounts of it – would be a proper preparation for the heroic ordeal of trying to make sense of the *gorchanau*.

What has been attempted in this book is a presentation of these old words with, I hope, enough explanation and comment to make pertinent matters clear, in the hope that some of the emotional power of this classic work may be felt by the reader. Whatever may be the complicated history of the text – and the evidence for some core of the *Gododdin* belonging to the late sixth century is more than probable – we do have the poems, and that is the most important thing.

To turn to more mundane matters: the two main difficulties in translating this early material are that the meanings of some words are not known, and that some other words have several meanings. As to the latter, more than one of them may be appropriate in context, so I have chosen the meanings that seem to me to be most valid. There is, in addition to the usual difficulties of creating a correspondence to a work of literature in one language in another, the annoyance that words for the same objects are not of the same length in Welsh and English: this can create havoc with the rhythm. Then words that rhyme or are consonant in one language do not rhyme or have no consonance in another: this can seriously affect the auditory emotional impact of the verse. Finally, the associations that some words have accumulated over centuries in one language may not have the same associations in another. So why bother? There's no answer to that.

As with all attempts at translation it is proper that I acknowledge the translations of others and also, in this instance, the illuminating work of many scholars.

I wish to thank Dylan Williams and Marian Beech Hughes for reading this work and making very useful suggestions and comments, but what is printed is, of course, my own responsibility.

Gwyn Thomas
Bangor, October 2012

Abbreviations &c

IW: Ifor Williams

DH: Daniel Huws. See 'A Select Bibliography'.

R. indicates emendations to lines in the text where words do not make sense to me, or others; or where they make better sense with emendations. This information is meant only for those who may have a special interest in the Welsh text.

❋ indicates poems that are not part of the 'basic' *Gododdin* text.

The names of warriors in the *Gododdin* odes are printed in a **heavier type**.

Italics in a translation indicate a tentative attempt at making sense of the original, or words that are probably not an inherent part of the poem.

Gododdin

1   MANUSCRIPT PAGE: 1.1–9, A TEXT

In might, a man: the age span of a lad;
In war, [a warrior] full of valour.
Swift horses, coarse-maned
Beneath his thighs – this handsome youth.
A light, broad shield
On the crupper of his steed;
Blue, beautiful swords
With fringes, gold-embroidered.
There won't be, there will never be
Between you and me
Any enmity;
Rather will there be
To you from me
A song in your praise.
Sooner to battle he
Than to any wedding;
Sooner to be
Food for crows
Than to a formal burial.
Owain, a dear friend to me,
It is a great shame that he
Is now under stones.[1]

[continued overleaf...]

---

1 R. fain

It's a wonder to me
That in any land he,
The only **son of Marro**,
Could be killed.[1]

2   MANUSCRIPT PAGE: 1.10–15, A TEXT

Torque-wearer,[2] front-warrior wherever he went;
Before a maid – breathless: but well worth his mead!
The face of his shield was shattered;
Wherever he heard any war-cry,
To all those he pursued
He'd never show mercy:
He'd not go from battle till the blood flowed,
Like reeds he mowed down the men who'd not flee.
The men of Gododdin in the hall tell:[3]
"Before **Madog**'s tent, on return from attack,
Just one of a hundred would not with him come back."[4]

---

1 The *Gododdin* frequently refers to warriors who did not have a formal burial, meaning that they died on the field of battle – they died with their boots on. This is a topos or a eulogistic commonplace in this poetry.

2 The epithet 'torque-wearer' occurs several times in this poetry. Kenneth Jackson chooses to translate the original Welsh *caeawg* as 'wearing a brooch' – that is, a large penannular type of brooch, since diadems or coronets 'appear to have been quite unknown among the Celtic peoples in the Dark Ages'. The earlier Celtic warriors wore torques, or gold collars. Among the Celts the torque signified honour and nobility, and even divinity. The suggestion that *torque-wearer* is an 'empty formula of archaic origin preserved in the poetry' is an excellent one – apart from the key word 'empty'. This is an archaic formula that has rich connotations and resonance within this ancient bardic praise tradition.

3 R. neus

4 R. ni

Torque-wearer, warrior, enemy-ensnarer:
His swooping – like an eagle in estuaries feeding![1]
Point by point to his pledge exactly adhering,
He exceeded his purpose – never was there any flinching.
Before the host of Gododdin there was a great fleeing
On the land of Manawyd,[2] by mighty compelling:
Neither armour nor shield was of use in protecting.
No-one could, without a [true] warrior's training,
Avoid the blow of **Cadfannan.**

---

1 The poet must have seen ospreys, closing their wings and swooping down with great speed to catch fish.

2 Manawyd may be the name of a man from Manaw: either the Isle of Man, or a territory near the head of the Firth of Forth. The poem refers to fighting in some territory other than Catraeth.

Torque-wearer, front-warrior, a wolf in a fray;
For his spoil, the torque-wearer seized amber beads.[1]
For his cup full of wine, of great worth was **Gwefrawr**.[2]
He thrust back all attacks, with blood on his cheek.
Though Gwynedd-men and Northmen should come to his land
    By the scheming of the **son of Ysgyrran**,
      Shields were all shattered!

5   MANUSCRIPT PAGE: 2.5–12, A TEXT

Torque-wearer, front-warrior, armed in the fighting,
Before his time came, mighty in the clashing of armies,
A leader in front of armies, there striking –
Before his blades five fifties falling!
There fell, of the men of Deira and men of Bernicia,
A hundred score at one time to oblivion.
Sooner he to be flesh for a wolf than a wedding,[3]
Sooner gain for a crow than to any altar;
Before his obsequies, his blood to the ground flowed
In payment for mead in a hall with the hosts;
Hyfaidd Hir will be praised whilst any poet's still singing.

---

1 R. goddiwawdd
2 The name of the hero, Gwefrawr, means 'amber beads'.
3 To die on the battlefield, without a formal burial, and to be preyed on by wolves or crows was honourable. To die young, before being married or having a dowry, was also honourable.

Warriors went to Gododdin, with banter and laughing:
Bitter in battle, with spears in ranks forming.
One short year: they're now at peace, they are now silent!
The **son of Bodgad** – the deeds of his hands wrought slaughter.
Though they went to churches[1] for penance,
Old and young, the strong and the lowly,
That sure encounter with death came upon them.

7   MANUSCRIPT PAGE: 2.18–20, A TEXT

Warriors went to Gododdin with fierce laughing,
In a band they're attackers, in war unrelenting,
They killed with blades with no loud clamouring;
Rheithfyw, pillar of battle, delighted in giving.

---

1 The reference to churches suggests that this was, nominally, a Christian
society. This type of Christian sentiment is not inconsistent with the mores of
a heroic age. But it has been suggested that such references may be additions to
the *Gododdin* proper.

Warriors went to Catraeth, a ready host,
Fresh mead[1] their feast, but it became bitter.
Three hundred warriors under orders fighting.
And after the joyfulness, there was silence.
Though they went to churches for penance,
That sure encounter with death came upon them.

9   MANUSCRIPT PAGE: 3.3–9, A TEXT

Warriors went to Catraeth, a mead-reared host,
Powerful, mighty – a shame not to name them,
With blood-red blades, very large in dark sockets.
Tightly and grimly the dogs of war fought.
On the host of Bernicia I'd have deemed them a burden –
Not one in man's semblance would I alive leave!
I've lost a friend (unwav'ring was I),
He was swift in advancing: hard is it to leave him.
The hero did not seek any bride-father's dowry,
The dear **son of Cian**, [who came] from Maen Gwynngwn.[2]

---

1 Mead is made from honey and is a bright yellow liquid. Kenneth Jackson notes, with astute perception, that it 'tastes of honey with a sweet first impression and a slight but distinct aftertaste of bitterness'. The sweetness and the bitterness are used literally and metaphorically in this *awdl*.
2 Maen Gwynngwn is a place, somewhere in Pictland, for Cian came from 'over the Bannawg', or Bannock, see Ode 22B.

Warriors went to Catraeth, they went with the dawn;
All of their fears were lifted away.
A hundred thousand with three hundred[1] clashing!
Spears were stained, [stained red] with blood.
His station in battle was, of all, the most valiant
At the front of the host of Mynyddawg Mwynfawr.

Warriors went to Catraeth with the dawn of the day.
Their [valorous] nature cut their lives short.
They drank mead – yellow and sweet, and ensnaring.
For a year many a singer was joyful.
Red their swords; let their spears not be washed –
White-enamelled,[2] with heads in four segments –
At the front of the host of Mynyddawg Mwynfawr.

---

1 Three hundred men attacking 100,000 is the kind of exaggeration that can be expected in this type of heroic song, unless it is a display of – unwarranted – optimism.
2 Enamel may refer to decoration, or to a 'chalked shield'. The four notches means that the spear point was not flat, so that if one were looking down on it, it would be a cross, +.

Warriors went to Catraeth at the break of day.
He put [mighty] armies to shame.
With their blades, full of doom, they made it
Necessary, in the world, to have biers.
Before "Peace" was declared, he caused
A bloodbath, brought death to his foe.
In the front of the army of [the men of] Gododdin,
When **Neirthiad**, [a warrior] of valiant intent,
Made any move he brought about glory.

A warrior went to Catraeth with the dawning of day,
Every mid-night he drank draughts of mead.[1]
Full of grief, a lament for an army
Was his onslaught, most impassioned of killers.

No great man attacked
At Catraeth who was
More generous of purpose
Over the mead.[2]
From the fort of Eidyn,
No one scattered the enemy
So thoroughly as he.

Tudfwlch Hir away from his homesteads, away from his land –
He slaughtered Saxons[3] all the days of the week.
His valour will endure and his memory
Long among his fair companions.
When **Tudfwlch**,[4] strong man of his people,
Son of Cilydd came, the station
Of spears was a station of blood.

---

1 R. neu
2 R. odd uch medd
3 Note that the enemy is here, and elsewhere, called 'Saxons' (*Saeson*) [43B, 45A, 45B, 54A]. The men of Bernicia and Deira are usually named as the enemy in the *Gododdin*. It has been assumed that about the year 600, the tribes of Bernicia and Deira were Angles – a name that is used in the *Gorchan of Cynfelyn*. Why call the enemy Saxons? Kenneth Jackson has suggested that 'the early Welsh used *Saeson* in general of all their Anglo-Saxon enemies'. In 44A and 94 the land of the enemy is *Lloegr* meaning 'England'.
4 The splitting of a name – Tudfwlch . . . son of Cilydd – is common in Welsh poetry. The technical term for this is *trychiad*, which can be translated as 'incision'.

A warrior went to Catraeth with the dawn
In his stronghold of shields, all interlinked[1]
It was savagely they attacked [and] collected booty;
Loud, like thunder, was the clashing of shields.
Haughty man, wise warrior, a champion,
He hacked and thrust forward with [his] lances.
Above bloody wounds, with blades he struck,
In the harshness of war:
There were iron weapons upon [warriors'] heads.
In the hall, this killer made his obeisance:
[But] before **Erthgi**[2] [great] armies lay groaning.

1 R. yn ei fuddyn
2 'Erthgi' is a compound of *arth* (a bear) and *ci* (dog).

15   MANUSCRIPT PAGE: 4.16–22, A TEXT

Of the land of Catraeth it is told
That hosts fell: for them, the lamenting is long.
Easy or hard, they defended their land
Against the sons (wicked clan) of Godebog.[1]
Long biers carried off the blood-splashed warriors.
A wretched fate (battle-faithful)[2] it was
That was ordained for **Tudfwlch** and **Cyfwlch Hir.**
Though we drank glowing mead by the light of reed-tapers,
Though its taste was sweet, its bitterness was long.

16   MANUSCRIPT PAGE: 5.1–7, A TEXT

Blaen, from the bright fort of Eidyn,[3]
Inspired faithful warriors who would follow him.
Blaen, on a cushion of feathers, would hand out
The horn in his opulent court.
Blaen, a draught of bragget made its way to him!
Blaen took delight in purple and gold;
Blaen, horses – well fed – ran under him
In the clamour of battle: for resolve he deserved them.
Blaen raised a war-cry, "A tide of great booty!"
A bear on a pathway, always late to retreat.

---

1 Godebog may refer to the tribe of Coel (King Cole). The *awdl* refers to a battle where Britons fought against Britons. Or the words, *gwerin enwir,* translated here as 'wicked clan' may mean quite the opposite, 'loyal tribe'.

2 In Welsh, the words in round brackets are called *sangiadau*, that is, words 'trodden in'. They are interpolations which are, in this ode, relevant comments on the topics mentioned.

3 R. ech Eidyn

Might in the front,
Sunlight on grass.
Lord, where can the heaven
Of Britain be found?
Rough the ford before a warrior;
His shield is a stronghold;
His drinking-horn splendid
In the [great] hall of Eidyn.
His majesty was displayed,
His mead intoxicating.
He drank strong wine,
Was savage in reaping;
He drank glowing wine,
Was audacious in war,
The battle-leek reaper,
Bright battle-kindler.
They sang a war-song,
Were armed in battle,
Were winged in battle.
Not undamaged his shield
By the lances of war;
Companions fell
In the clashes of battle.
Not weak was his war-cry,
Without fault he avenged them:
His fury was appeased
Before a cover of green
Was seen on the grave of
Gwrfelling the Great.

They revere lawful rights,
They stain their three spears
[In the blood of] fifty and five hundred.
Three war-hounds – with three hundred –
Three war-horsemen
Gold-mantled from Eidyn,
Three armies in mail-coats,
Three kings golden-torqued,
Three violent horsemen,
Three equals in battle,
Three peers together
In unison bounding;
With harshness they routed the foe.
Three oppressive in war,
With ease did they slaughter in battle,
Golden were they in any tight fighting;
Three kings of hosts
Who came from the Brython –
Cynri and **Cynon**,
[And] **Cynrain** of Aeron.[1]
The scheming tribesmen,
[Those men] of Deira, they used to ask:
"Came there from the Brython
A better man than **Cynon**;
A serpent, the sting of [his] foes?"

---

1 Aeron: could it be Ayr, a river; or Earn, in Renfrewshire; or Ayrshire?

I drank wine and mead in the hall.
   The number of his spears were many,
   In the onslaught of warriors
      He provided food for eagles!
When **Cydywal** attacked, a war-cry arose
With the green dawn; wherever he came,
He left shields shattered [and shields] splintered.
      In battle – this ripper – he smashed
         Savage spears,
      He crushed the front of any army.
The **son of Sywno** – soothsayer [well] knew it –
      Sold his life
      For proclaiming of honour:
         He killed men with a sharpened blade;
He killed both Athrwys and Affrai.
For the sake of [his] pledge he planned to attack,
      He brought forth the corpses
      Of ferocious warriors:
         He thrust in front of [the warriors of] Gwynedd.

20A   MANUSCRIPT PAGE: 6.13-16, A TEXT

You drank wine and mead in the hall;[1]
Since you drank (woeful fate!), you attacked in the marches.
Your valorous heart was not without havoc!
When all others attacked, you would attack.
May you have glory, for you did not sin.
Brave **Breichiawr** was the talk of the world.

20B   MANUSCRIPT PAGE: 31.12-17, B TEXT

Splendid, well-nurtured, at [war] you excelled.
Many spears there were when you hastened forth.
When all [others] fled, you would attack.
If the blood of the dead that you killed were wine
You would have enough for three or four years.[2]
Greatly would you, for your steward, reduce it!
May there be a place for thee in Heaven
Because you would never flee.
Tenacious **Breichiawl**, the talk of the world.

---

1 R. yfaist
2 R. meddud; lit. *three and four*

Warriors went to Catraeth, they were famous;
From vessels of gold, for a whole year,
Their liquor was wine and was mead,
In keeping with an honoured custom,
Three men and three score and three hundred,[1] gold-torqued.
Of those that attacked after plentiful wine,
Only three got away through valour in combat:
The two war-hounds of Aeron,[2] and **Cynon** came back,[3]
And – from my blood-shedding – I
For the sake of my excellent song.

---

1 In some of the *awdlau* the number in the host is 300; in others – as here – it
is 363. Here 3 warriors and the poet returned form the slaughter at Catraeth.
2 Aeron: see Ode 18.
3 R. daerawd < daeredaf

22A   MANUSCRIPT PAGE: 7.1–5, A TEXT

My kinsman in carousal caused us no distress
Except on account of the hard dragon's feast.[1]
He wasn't kept back from the mead in the hall:
This assailant – he caused havoc on havoc,
Was audacious in battle, audacious in action.
The men of Gododdin, after battle, recount
That no one was sharper than **Llifiau**.[2]

22B   MANUSCRIPT PAGES: 31.18–32.2, B TEXT

When he attacked on the frontier he was of great fame;
He was worthy of wine – this gold-torqued warrior.
He marshalled a bright, shining line of the brave,
The noble one led one hundred warriors;
Illustrious of nature, a foreigner-horseman,
From over the Bannawg, **only son of Cian**.
On the field of battle, Gododdin men do not say[3]
That anyone was sharper than **Llif**.

---

1 R. durawd; dragon, *a metaphor for a warrior*
2 *llifio* means to sharpen; to saw
3 R. nis adrawdd

23A   MANUSCRIPT PAGE: 7.6–10, A TEXT

Weapons scattered,
Ranks all broken, [and] he standing steadfast.
With great destruction
The champion smashed the English rabble.
He sowed spears
In the front rank of battle, in the fighting with lances.[1]
Before his death
He laid men low, made women widows.
Graid son of Hoywgi
With spears causing bloodshed.

23B   MANUSCRIPT PAGE: 31.7–11, B TEXT

In front of the ford he, for armies, bore pressure,
[In] the mighty array of battle,[2]
Splendid attacker, brilliant of mind,[3]
His fate was not of any ill omen:[4]
I've heard, in song, of his great good fortune.
Before his death
He laid men low,
He made women widows.
Braint son of Bleiddgi
With spears causing bloodshed.[5]

---

1 R. trais
2 R. dull; cedyr, *plural of* cadr
3 R. gorleu
4 DH: lam *not* llain = Not awkward his spears
5 R. ac

Hero with protective shield, beneath its speckled boss,[1]
And like a young colt trotting;
He was the tumult of hill warfare, was a fire blazing;
His spears went speeding, like the sun was he:
Now food for ravens, of some use for a crow.
But before he was left [there] at the fords
With the fall of the dew [upon him], and the wave breaking
On his breast, he was an eagle, graceful in flight:
World's bards assess great-hearted men.
His counsels deprived him of his proper rights,
His chief warriors were trashed by the foe;
But before he was buried beneath Eleirch Fre[2] –
          In his heart there was valour.
His blood washed over his armour:
Buddfan son of Bleiddfan, undaunted!

---

1 R. ardwy
2 Eleirch Fre = the Hill of Swans

It would be wrong to leave him unremembered,
The one of mighty exploits. He'd not leave
Any breach [in the ranks] for cowardice.
He – benefactor of the minstrelsy[1]
Of Britain – did not leave his court
On purpose on New Year's Day.[2]
His land was not ploughed, though it lay waste.
Most hostile in battle, [most] generous dragon;
A dragon in bloodshed after the wine-feast –
Gwenabwy son of Gwen, in the encounter at Catraeth.

26A   MANUSCRIPT PAGE: 8.2–7, A TEXT

It was true, as **Cadlew** declared:[3]
"No man's horses ever caught **Marchlew**."
In battle he sowed spears
From a bounding, [and] wide-charging [steed].
Though not brought up with pain or burdens
His sword-thrust was vicious in his battle-station.
He sowed ash[-spears] from the four clefts[4]
Of his hand on his steaming, slender, auburn [horse].
He'd give – this most beloved – of his great store of wine:
He'd strike with a blade, blood-stained and savage.
As reapers mow in changing weather,
So **Marchlew** caused great flows of blood.

---

1 R. cerddwriaeth
2 If any man left his court on New Year's Day that meant he was not generous.
The poets regarded a lack of generosity as a cardinal sin – if not *the* cardinal sin.
3 R. amceuddai
4 The four clefts of his hand are the four spaces between the fingers of a hand.

Tudlew told you, with false words,
That no man's steed caught **Marchlew**.
Though not brought up with pains and burdens,
His sword-thrust was mighty in his station in battle.[1]
Profusely he'd scatter his spears of ash
From the four clefts of his hand from a horse
That was dappled and slender and steaming.

27   MANUSCRIPT PAGE: 8.8–11, A TEXT

Isag,[2] most courteous, he came from the south;
Like the flow of the sea were his customs
For modesty, generosity
And the fine drinking of mead.
Where his weapons smite
He'd let vengeance elapse.
He was not ever ferocious and then not ferocious,
Was not ever certain and then was uncertain.
His sword kept resounding in the heads of mothers!
Rampart of battle, **son of Gwyddnau** was praised.

---

1 R. yn ei orth
2 Isag is a biblical name.

Ceredig, well-loved was his fame,
He seized his glory and retained it.
A favourite son, he was so gentle
Before his day[1] came:
Most excellent his courtesy.
May the beloved of hosts be appointed
A time in the land of Heaven, the home of acclaim.

Ceredig, a leader well-loved,
A most dangerous champion in combat,
Gold-adorned shield of the field of battle,
He shattered spears and splintered spears.
Ferocious and mighty his sword-thrust,
Like a hero he protected the station of spears.
Before earth's sorrow, before suffering,
With forethought he defended his post.
May he be welcomed among the Host of Heaven,
With the Trinity[2] in immaculate union.

---

1 His day = the day of his death; before his time came.
2 As in other *awdlau* there are references to Christian beliefs here.

When **Caradog** rushed forth into battle
Like a wild boar – a killer of thirty,
Bull of an army, a slayer in combat –
He'd feed the [wild] wolves with his hand.
My witness is **Owain, son of Eulad,**
And **Gwrien** and **Gwyn** and **Gwriad.**[1]
From Catraeth, from the slaughter,
From Bryn Hyddwn before it was taken –
After bright mead [held] in the hand –
Not one man of them saw his father [again].

Warriors charged, leapt forward together:
[All were] short-lived,
[All were] drunk over clarified mead,
The men of Mynyddawg, so glorious in battle –
Their lives were their payment for their feasting on mead:
Caradawg, Madawg, Pyll and **Ieuan,**
Gwgawn and **Gwiawn, Gwyn** and **Cynfan,**
Peredur Steel-weapons, Gwawrddur and **Aeddan:**
Attackers in battle, all shattered their shields!
And though they were slain, they themselves slew:
Not one to his homeland returned.

---

1 The names of the last three heroes in this ode occur together as 'Gwen a Gwrien a Gwriad' in one of the Stanzas of the Graves, *Englynion Beddau*, in the Black Book of Carmarthen.

Warriors attacked, they'd been nurtured together
Over mead for a year; how great their intent.
How sad is their story – with unfulfilled longing!
Their resting place is cruel, no man gave them succour.
How long the longing for them, [how long] the lamenting,
For the splendid warriors from wine-nurtured land:
Gwlged[1] of Gododdin, for men [ever] ready,
Arranged the famous, the costly feast of Mynyddawg
To redeem the land of Catraeth.

33   MANUSCRIPT PAGE: 9.16–21, A TEXT

Warriors went to Catraeth in an army, with war-cries,
A force of steeds with dark armour and shields,
[With] lances held high and sharp spears,
And swords and shining mail-shirts.
He took the lead, he hacked through armies,
Five fifties fell before his blades –
Rhufawn Hir: he gave gold to the altar,
And gifts and fine presents to a singer.

---

1 Gwlged (or Gwlyged; Gwlgod or Gwlygod) appears to be Mynyddawg's
steward, the man in charge of the feasting in Eidyn.

No hall was ever so renowned:
So great, so enormous its slaughter!
Fiery **Morien**, you deserved your mead.
Cynon did not say he'd not make a corpse –
An armoured spearman of far-reaching fame.
His sword resounded to the end of the rampart.
No more can a stone of great compass be budged[1]
Than **Gwid son of Peithan** be shifted.

No hall was ever made so famous.
Except for **Morien, son of Caradawg**,
No bold warrior, like a lord, escaped in battle[2]
Who was bolder than the **son of Fferrawg**.
Strong his hand – he drew sparks[3] from a fleeing horseman!
Bold one in battle, a city to a timorous army,
In the front of the host of Gododdin, his shield
Was shattered; under stress he was steadfast.
On the day of battle, he was lively: his recompense was bitter;
Mynyddawg's liegeman – he deserved his mead-horns.

---

1 R. nog y cysgyg
2 R. nid engis
3 The flight was fast enough to create sparks.

No hall was ever made so mighty.
[LOST LINE]
Than **Cynon**, generous of heart, a lord adorned.
It was he who would sit at the end of a bench:[1]
Whoever he thrust need not be thrust twice!
The points of his spears were especially sharp;
With shattered shield he tore into armies;
Very swift were his horses; he charged in the front.
On the day of battle his blades were destructive
When, with the green dawn, **Cynon** attacked.

No hall was ever made so faultless, or
[A lord] so liberal, so lion-like in fury,
So widely travelled as **Cynon**,
Of fairest nobility, with a generous heart;
A citadel in battle on the farthest of flanks,
A door, army's anchor, most noble in worth
Of those that I've seen and shall see in battle
Bearing arms; the greatest his valour in combat.
He killed the foe with the sharpest of blades,
Like rushes they fell by his hand.
Son of Clydno of enduring fame, I'll sing praise,[2]
Lord, to you without end, without limit.

---

1 R. neud
2 R. it iôr

He attacked in battle in the front line,
Drove out the foe, set up the border;
A spear-thrusting lord, laughing in combat;
Like **Elffin**,[1] with valour he rushed forward,
The famous **Eithinyn**, bull of battle, rampart in war.

39A   MANUSCRIPT PAGE: 10.20–23, A TEXT

He attacked in battle in the front line
For mead in the hall and a draught of wine.
He sowed his blades between two armies,
A magnificent horseman before Gododdin
Was the famous **Eithinyn**,
Bull of battle, rampart in war.

39B   MANUSCRIPT PAGE: 14.7–11, A TEXT

There was an uprising of skilled, mighty warriors
To [go to] Catraeth, a swift, ready army,
In return for mead in the hall and a draught of wine.
He sowed his blades between two armies,
A magnificent horseman before Gododdin,
Bull of battle, the famous **Eithinyn**.

---

1 We know nothing of this Elffin [from Alpinus > Alpine].

For the cattle-herds of the east[1]
In battle like a wild beast
He attacked: I honour him.
In payment for the mead,
Of the greatest valour,
Splendid and lucky, [and] a brilliant leader
Was the **son of Boddw Addaf**, the famous **Eithinyn**.

Mighty warriors went from among us,
They'd been nurtured on mead and on wine.
    Because of the feast of Mynyddawg
    I'm [full] of sorrow[2]
        For the loss of a tough man of war.
    Like the sound of thunder
    Was the sound of shields' clatter[3]
        Before the attack of **Eithinyn**.

---

1 R. dwyrain
2 R. handwyf
3 R. ef

He attacked in battle for the herds of the east;[1]
A host arose, with [their] shields hanging.[2]
With shattered shield was he
Leading the cattle, **Beli Bloeddfawr.**[3]
Above [all the] blood, a lord
Making haste for the border,
A warrior, grey-haired, he sustained us
On a leading, lively horse,
He was rugged of shape, an ox, [and] gold-torqued.
The boar made a pledge before
That treacherous border,
[He was] worth his rights, a battle repulser.
"He who calls us to Heaven let Him be,
In war, a protector!"
He brandished his spears in combat.
Cadfannan of great fame, he gathered booty;
There was no fighting in which he,
The champion, did not have an army.

1 R. dwyrain
2 A hanging shield is one that is hung by its straps, not one that is held in the warrior's hand ready for action.
3 *Bloeddfawr* means 'loud shout'.

For the battle, for the land there's great sorrow,
For the fair land, for the land laid waste,
For the fall of hair from the head,
For the warriors of the eagle, **Gwyddien**:
Fiercely he defended them with his spear,
[The land's] ruler, its cultivator, its owner.
Morien defended
The fair song of Myrddin,[1] and laid the head
Of the chieftain in earth, with our help and our support.[2]
Bradwen [fought like] three men for a maiden's favour;
Gwenabwy son of Gwên, [he fought like] twelve.

---

1 Myrddin (Merlin): a poet, a prophet. Later he became a major figure in the Arthurian legend.
2 R. a chamen

[CORRUPT TEXT]
For the battle, for the land there's great sorrow,
For the fair land, for the land laid waste.
Three sixes bearded, in battle weak [and] skulking[1] –
Morien brought [them] with his spear.[2]
A noisy defence of an army,[3]
Against Saxons and Irish and Picts.[4]
Well-loved was the stiff corpse, [was] the white cheek
Of the skilled **son of Gwên, Gwenafwy.**

---

1 R. tri chwe barfawd drais, dilib lechen; llib: llibin = *weak*; llech cf. llechu = *hiding-place*, *skulker*.
2 R. adwgai; gwialen
3 R. argae = *defence*; freuer = *noisy*; bragaden = *army*
4 R. at gynt; Pryden. Note that the hero in this ode had been fighting against Saxons, Irish and Picts.

For the battle, for the land there's great sorrow.
The shields were of use in the battle,
In the conflict there was
A sword-blow on a head,
In Lloegr[1] [there were] damaged men
Before three hundred lords.
He who would hold a wolf's mane[2]
Without even a staff in his hand –
It is usual for such a man to have,
Beneath his mantle, a splendid spirit!
    In the encounter of loss and ferocity
    Bradwen died, he didn't escape.

---

1 *Lloegr* is the Welsh word for England.
2 Does this episode about killing a wolf recall the story of the young David who became king of Israel, see I Samuel 17.34–7.

[CORRUPT TEXT]
For the feast, for rough land there's great sorrow,
For the dense, for the heavy, the very waste land.
A heroic lord,[1]
A hero bearded, speckled of wing
Looks at Eidyn and the land.
Very splendid his hand in a gauntlet
Against heathens and Irish and Picts.
He who may feel a wolf's mane[2]
Without even a staff in his hand,
It is usual for such a man to have,
In his mantle, mighty fury!
    I shall sing that **Morien** may not die,
    The right hand of **Gwenabwy, the son of Gwên.**

---

1 R. camhunben
2 R. glywo

[CORRUPT TEXT]
Gold on the wall of a fort,
A brilliant attack,[1]
A raid on a settlement,[2]
[With the] intense tumult of war,
A Saxon and his shouting.[3]
Birds were fed,[4]
In the hurly-burly of battle.
No one living can tell[5]
What befell the leader,[6]
    And of his fiery nature.[7]
No one living in the hour of sorrows says[8]
That **Cynhafal** was not a protector.[9]

---

1 R. claer
2 R. *as in* 'dygredu'; aer-floddiad
3 R. un saxo a'i leisiar
4 R. gofwydwyd
5 R. Nis adrodd a fo fyw
6 R. o ddamweiniaid llyw
7 R. odd amluch lafanad
8 R. nis; byw; pleingiaid = *sorrows*
9 R. cynheilwad

Gold on the wall of a fort,
An attack in battle,
A raid on a settlement,
[With the] intense tumult of war.
A Saxon became prey,
He was of use to birds[1]
In the land of [mead-]horns [and] pretty apparel.
No one alive says [anything]
About the leader of weak men.
About the form of one of a fiery nature
No one alive in the day of sorrows says
That **Cynhafal** was not a protector.

45C   MANUSCRIPT PAGE: 37.2–6, B TEXT

A most fierce, conspicuous warrior,[2]
A fine defender,
Rapid, not gentle in war;
A battle feast[3] –
A varied feast . . . a trampler,[4]
A battle-lion, highly skilled;[5]
Most excellent,[6]
Of most commendable ambitions.[7]
Gododdin does not tell, on the day of battle,
That **Cynhafal** was not a protector.

---

1 R. gofuddiwyd
2 R. chwitrefydd claer
3 R. gwanar saig
4 R. amsut; sang
5 R. cadleo; gogyfrudd
6 R. gogyfrad
7 R. eddyli wy bwyllad

When you, a warrior of renown,
Were seizing corn on the frontiers,
We were, with reason,
Called illustrious, [and] men of distinction.
He was a mighty door, a mighty refuge,
He was courteous to those
Who resolutely sought him,
He was a fortress to any army that trusted him.
Where he was not, was not called blessed.

* 47   MANUSCRIPT PAGE: 12.7–8, A TEXT[1]

Cyd bai can ŵr yn un tŷ
Adwen ofalon Ceni
Pen gwŷr, tal bainc a deli.

Though there might be a hundred in a house
I know the anxieties of Cyny,
Chief of men, entitled to be
At the head of any bench.

---

1 This is an englyn from the Llywarch Hen cycle: *Canu Llywarch Hen,* 8; 98–9.

I am a weary lord,[1]
I don't settle any scores,
I laugh no laugh
Beneath the feet of hairy crawlers;
My knee's stretched out
In a house of earth,
[There is] an iron chain
About my knees.
For mead from a horn,
For the men of Catraeth
I, yet not I, **Aneirin**
(Taliesin knows it,
He of most mighty words)
Sang the *Gododdin*[2]
Before the dawn
Of the following day.

---

1 The speaker here appears to be Aneirin. Is this ode and Ode 49 an addition
to the text? Taliesin was another great *cynfardd* or 'first poet'. Morfydd E. Owen
has suggested that this ode and the next are not part of the original *Gododdin*,
but belong to a saga about Aneirin.

   R. neud. In the first line I have emended the negative *nid* to the positive *neud*.
If 'Aneirin' is in the predicament he describes, he could hardly be full of energy.
2 R. ceint

The glory of the North – a warrior achieved it;
Generous of heart, a lord [who was]
By nature bountiful;
None travels the earth, no mother gave birth
To one as handsome, as powerful, in his iron armour.
By the might of his shining sword he saved me,
From a cruel prison in the earth he took me,
From the place of death, from a hostile land –
Cenau son of Llywarch, undaunted [and] bold.[1]

The high court of **Senyllt**, with [all] its vessels
[Brim] full of mead, endured no shame.
He assigned the wicked to the sword,
He assigned invasions to war;
He carried the wounded away in his arms
Before the army of Bernicia and Deira.
It was usual to have in his court
Swift horses, dark armour, and blood.
[With] a long, yellow spear in his hand
In his wrath he would rush forth.
For a while smiling, for a while frowning,
[He was] unkind and kind by turns.
[With] warriors not used to showing
Their feet in fleeing,
Heilyn was a saviour on every border.

---

1 If the 'me' is Aneirin, he has been saved 'from a cruel prison' by Cenau.

[CORRUPT TEXT]
A rock in open land, open land on a hill[1]
On the border of Gododdin,
The warring borderland;[2]
The war counsel [was][3]
For battle upon open land,[4]
[With] fair spear[s].[5]
If this were well arranged
In the time of tempest,
Tempest time
[Would] bring a rank led by a champion.
From Dindywyd
There came to us [a host]
In tight ranks, with one another pleading,
Sharply they thrust, thoroughly did they attack.[6]
The shield of **Grugyn** – its front was shattered
Before the bull of battle.

---

1 R. llech leutud tudleu fre
2 R. ystre argad
3 R. argad
4 R. leufre
5 R. cangen = *spear*
6 R. gwenyn

A rock in open land, in open land a hill
On the border of Gododdin,
The warring borderland.
The war counsel[1]
Was a counsel about a tempest,
About a vessel from over the sea,
About a host from over the sea,
A very weak host;
A very weak, a mongrel host
From Dindywyd
Came to us;
The shield of **Grugyn**, its front was shattered
Before the bull of battle.

---

1 R. argad

A rock in open land,[1]
With [upon it] snakelike motion,
The motion of a dragon.[2]
There was fair play before Gododdin
[Upon] the Strand of Annon.
He brought luxury
From the wine tents for the good of the land.
The time of tempests –
Vessels from over the sea,
A host from over the sea,
A host of deceivers.
A fine, swift battalion before a king's host
From Dindywyd
Came to us, happened upon us.
The shield of **Grugyn** – its front was shattered
In front of the loop in the river
Where there was war.

---

1 R. lleudir
2 R. sarffgar duth duth dragon

His weapon makes his enemies tremble,
A fierce eagle, in battle laughing loudly.
His spears are sharp around Bancarw,
The fingers of the freckled man [can] crush a head!
[A man] of many moods – boisterous [or] pleasant;
[A man] of many moods – thoughtful [or] laughing aloud;
Rhys squandered with vigour, ostentation and speed;[1]
Not so those who will not achieve their purpose.
Those whom he may chance to overtake
Can not escape.

It was not by good luck that the shield
Of **Cynwal** the kindly was pierced;
It was not by good luck that he set his thigh
On a slender, grey [steed] with long legs;
Yellow his spear, yellow;[2]
[Yet] yellower his saddle.
Your man's in his cell[3]
Gnawing the leg of a buck;
The spoils in his hand –
May that be very rare for him!

---

1 R. ysbrowys; rhodres
2 yellow, *that is*, 'yellow with wear'
3 R. dy ŵr

54A   MANUSCRIPT PAGES: 13.13–14.1, A TEXT

It was good that **Addonwy** came.[1]
Gently you had promised me –
What **Bradwen** would do, you would do:[2]
You would kill, you would burn;
You'd do no worse than **Morien**.
You did not hold the wing
[Of the army] or the front line.
[Though] your eye was bold and open
You did not see the great swelling fury of the horsemen:
They killed, they gave no quarter to the Saxons.

54B   MANUSCRIPT PAGE: 30.12–15, B TEXT

[CORRUPT TEXT]
It was a good gift, **Addonwy**,[3]
Addonwy that you promised me:
What **Bradwen** would do, you would do,
You would kill, you would burn.
You did not hold the wing
[Of the army] or the front line.
Bold is the township of your . . .
I did not see from the sea to the sea[4]
A horseman that was worse than your man.

---

1 Was Addonwy killed early in combat?
2 R. wnelai
3 R. dofod
4 We have the definite article in the text here, twice; very unusual.

Gododdin, I claim your support[1]
[In] the valleys beyond the ridges
Of Drum Esyd;[2]
[I], a young man, without constraint, seeking silver
With the advice of **the son of Dwywai,**
[And] your courage.

He was not weak of counsel,
[Was not] base before a blazing fire –
The pine alight from twilight to twilight,
[With] a doorway lit up to a pilgrim in purple.
The killing of the gentle one,
The killing of the splendid one, a rampart of battle –
Unseparable was his song and **Aneirin.**

---

1 Someone – a reciter, possibly? – seeks the support of Aneirin's *Gododdin*: this ode is not a part of the basic text.
2 Drum Esyd: an unidentified place. Aneirin was the son of Dwywai. She is mentioned as the daughter of Lleynnog. A Dwywai was also the mother of Deinioel, the saint and founder of Bangor. He died in 584.

Gododdin, I make claim on your behalf[1]
In the presence of a host in the hall, boldly!
And the song of the **son of Dwywai**
Of good courage – may it be famous
In the one place where it excels.
Since the gentle one, war rampart, was killed,
Since earth went over **Aneirin**
Now [his] song and Gododdin are parted.

56   MANUSCRIPT PAGE: 14.20–15.1, A TEXT

Warriors, men equal in status rose up,
Land's might – let their follower be heard.

The wave (that bright pilgrim) crashed down
Where they were, the lively lord[s].[2]
In a high hedge you'd hardly see the little twigs.[3]
A deserving chief makes no pact with provoking.
Morial, in pursuit, won't bear any fault[s] –
A steel blade that is ready for bloodshed.

---

1 Another version of one seeking the support of Aneirin.
2 R. elëin
3 R. o fre wrych gwelych: *a gnomic line*

57   MANUSCRIPT PAGE: 14.12–16, A TEXT

Warriors, men equal in status rose up,
Land's might – let their follower be heard.
He killed huge, fierce warriors
With cudgel and spears,
[And] the trampling of hooves.[1]

58   MANUSCRIPT PAGES: 14.20–15.2, A TEXT

Warriors arose, they gathered together;
Together, with one purpose, attacked.
Brief their lives: long the sorrow for them
Among those who loved them.
Seven times their number
They slew of the English.
By warfare they made widows,
Many a mother with tears at her eyelids.

---

1 R. carnawr

From the wine-feast and mead-feast
They dole out death.
How great was the status[1]
Of **Eiddol**, the unique.
In front of a hill,
Facing the hill of victory
He set crows soaring,
To the clouds ascending.
Warriors were upon him falling
Like a grey swarm
Without [forcing him]
[To anything] like a retreat.
[A man] of extensive, and sudden planning
Upon [steeds] whose snouts were pale,[2]
With thrusting sword upon a rampart.
The best man in the feast
Where there was no sleeping:
Today, he is unwaking –
The **son of Rheiddun**, a leader in battle.

---

1 R. mam > mor
2 *snouts*, lit. *lips*; R. gweilwon

From wine-feast and mead-feast, from us they went,
Mail-clad warriors; I know sorrow for their dying.[1]
Before their hair turned grey they were killed:
In front of Catraeth they were a lively host!
Of the retinue of Mynyddawg (great [is the] grief),
Of the three hundred, only one man came back.[2]

From wine-feast and mead-feast they went out to attack,
Warriors in combat, renowned, with no care for their lives;
In shining array, around a bowl, they drank together
Enjoying wine and mead and malt.[3]
For the host of Mynyddawg my mind's full of grief;[4]
Too many have I lost of my true kinsmen.
Of three hundred champions who rushed on Catraeth,
Alas, save for one man, no one came back.

---

1 R. neus
2 Here we are told that of the 300 only one man came back from Catraeth.
3 Malt: whiskey, of some sort.
4 R. handwyf adfant fy mryd

61B   MANUSCRIPT PAGE: 33.10–14, B TEXT

It was from the retinue of Mynyddawg
That they attacked;
It was in bright array, around a bowl,
That they together drank.
For the feast of Mynyddawg my mind's full of grief:
Too many have I lost of my true kinsmen.
Of three hundred gold-torqued who rushed on Catraeth,
Alas, save for one, no one escaped.

62   MANUSCRIPT PAGE: 16.3–6, A TEXT

Thus was he in the hosting,
Always like a ball on the bound,
Thus was he till returning.
Thus the men of Gododdin defended,
For wine and for mead, resolutely
In hardship on the frontier.
And under **Cadfannan** was a herd
Of red horses: a horseman,
In the morning ferocious.

Anchor, scatterer of Deira's warriors,
A serpent with a fearsome sting;
He would trample on dark armour
In the forefront of an army.
A terrifying bear,
A savage gate-keeper,
He'd trample on spears
On the day of the battle
In the alder-grown ditch.
Of **the seed of lord Neddig,**
He brought about, through [his] fury,
A feast for the birds
From the uproar of war.
For your faithful deed you are rightly called
Leader, lord, rampart of warriors:
Merin son of Madiain, you were born lucky.[1]

Anchor, scatterer of Deira's warriors,
A serpent with a fearsome sting
In the forefront of an army.
For your faithful deed you are rightly called
Ruler, leader, rampart of all armies:
Merin son of Madiaith, you were born lucky.

---

1 Born lucky: see the reference to this belief in the Introduction.

The water's very bright,[1]
Water is a grey wolf:
Battle follows . . .

Anchor, scatterer of Deira's warriors,
Immovable rock,
In the forefront of an army.
Many horses, many men
Are bloodied before
The warriors of Gododdin.
Swift dogs barking,[2]
A host arising,
[And] a defender in the thinning fog
In front of the headland of Merin.[3]

---

1 The section in italics does not appear to belong to the rest of the poem.
2 R. cŵn cyfarth
3 *Or*: Garth Merin.

Anchor, scatterer of Deira's warriors,
A serpent with a fearsome sting,
Immovable rock
Of the army's front line.
Of lively provision,[1]
Too violent for stress,[2]
Of outstanding desert
[In the] harshness of spears.
For your faithful deed you are rightly called
Ruler, leader, rampart of all nations,
Tudfwlch, the mighty in battle, a fortress barrier

---

1 R. arial
2 R. chymwy

Blades, blood-stained
Covering the ground,
A hero, high lord in battle,[1]
He leaps forward, this man-slayer;[2]
You would be happy
In the wolf-warrior's station, wolf of the host,
The war-band's herb garden,[3]
A killing champion:
Before he was caught, he wasn't a weakling![4]
For your faithful deed you are rightly called
Ruler, helmsman, rampart of all nations,
Tudfwlch, mighty in battle, a fortress barrier.

---

1 R. gorudd
2 DH: laim
3 Describing a hero as a 'herb garden' may not seem entirely appropriate to us, even if it did to an early audience. What we have here is a variation on the duality of the hero: he is a sustainer of his people – a veritable herb garden – but a destroyer of the enemy.
4 'caught', or 'made blind'

64A   MANUSCRIPT PAGE: 16.12–16, A TEXT

Singing, befitting a host, was delivered:
Our warriors went to war around Catraeth,
Tartan garments, blood-stained –
They were trampled;
The posts of war were trodden down
In vengeance for a payment of mead:
With corpses was this payment made.
Cibno does not tell, after the turmoil of battle
(Though he took communion [before it]),
That he received due payment.

64B   MANUSCRIPT PAGE: 38.9–14, B TEXT

Singing, befitting a host, was delivered:[1]
Our warriors went to war around Catraeth,
Tartan garments, blood-stained –
They were trampled;
The posts of war were trodden down
In vengeance for a payment of mead:
With corpses was this payment made.
Cibno does not tell, after the turmoil of battle,
(Though it was to him a communion)[2]
That he received due payment.

---

1 R. caffad
2 Communion, or 'his final rites'.

Fitting singing of a most noble host.
The sound of thunder and fire and flood-tide –
In the uproar of battle, he was
A horseman of excellent valour;
A blood-stained reaper,
He longed for war.
A violent warrior, he rushed to battle
In whatever land he heard it.
With his shield on his shoulder he'd pick up a spear
As he'd pick up sparkling wine in glass goblets.
About his mead he had silver:
It was gold that he deserved.
Gwaednerth son of Llywri –
He was brought up on wine.

66A   MANUSCRIPT PAGE: 17.1–5, A TEXT

The most fitting singing of brilliant hosts.
And after a flood a river abates.[1]
Beaks of grey eagles glorified his hand,[2]
He made food for carrion birds.
Of the gold torque-wearers who went to Catraeth
On the campaign of Mynyddawg, lord of hosts,
From the land of the Brython
There came, with no shame, to Gododdin
No man far better than **Cynon**.

---

1 DH: Aeron; R. a gwedi dyrraith dyfeinw afon
2 *beaks*: lit. *heads*

The most fitting singing to **Cynon**.
[Before] his laying out for burial in battle,[1]
And before the barrier of Aeron was lost
Beaks of grey eagles glorified his hand;
In fury he made food for carrion birds.
For the good of Mynyddawg, horseman of hosts,
He set his side against enemy spears.
In front of Catraeth warriors, gold-torqued,
They were eager –
They pierced, they killed [all] those who withstood them,
The whelps of wrath were far away from their land.
Rare was it in battle for any man of the Britons
Of Gododdin to be far better than **Cynon**.

The fitting singing of a skilful host.
He did not covet
A joyful little place in the world,
He sought, in the world about him,
The praise of poets
In return for gold and great horses,
And the drunkenness of mead.
But when he'd come back from battle,
[Then] blood-stained men
Praised [him], **Cynddilig of Aeron**.

---

1 R. cywair = *laying out for burial*

67B   MANUSCRIPT PAGE: 38.21–22, B TEXT

The most fitting singing of a skilful host.
A happy little place in the world, may you prosper ...

68   MANUSCRIPT PAGE: 17.10–13, A TEXT

The fitting singing of shining armies,
On the campaign of Mynyddawg, lord of hosts.
And the **daughter**[1] **of Eudaf Hir** –
She was clothed in purple,
Was Gwanannon's[2] oppressor,
A land of broken men.

---

1 Was the daughter of Eudaf Hir (Eudaf the Tall) the wife of Mynyddawg, as Ifor Williams suggested?
2 Gwanannon: probably a region on one of the borders of Gododdin. See Ode 74.

Half-men kept up the praise in the hall –
With the ferocity of a fire roaring when lit!
On Tuesday they put on their dark armour,[1]
On Wednesday their shields, lime-white, were prepared,
On Thursday their ruin was certain,
On Friday dead bodies were [there] brought forth,
On Saturday their action together was no burden,
On Sunday their red blades were brought,
On Monday blood-flow was seen, high as any man's thigh.
The men of Gododdin recount, after the fatigue [of combat],
Before the tent of **Madawg** when they came back:
"Apart from one man in a hundred,
No one returned."

---

1 The schedule of the battle is odd. Ifor Williams remarked that it was inappropriate that the warriors had put on their armour on a Tuesday, and received their weapons on a Wednesday. Kenneth Jackson says that this account 'can hardly mean that the battle lasted from Friday to Monday . . . if the tactic was a sudden shock attack by a tiny force of cavalry. More likely the whole thing is anticipatory till Monday'. But how a force of 300 men and, more than likely, some retainers, could travel down from Edinburgh to Catterick without being discovered is a mystery, as is the 'sudden shock attack'.

The stewards did not keep up the praise in the hall:
Because of the battle host, battle broke out
Like a roaring fire through kindling.
On Tuesday they put on their fair garments,
On Wednesday their common desire was bitter,
On Thursday envoys were pledged,
On Friday the corpses were counted,
On Saturday their action together was no burden,
On Sunday red blades were brought forth,
On Monday blood-flow was seen, high as any man's thigh.
The men of Gododdin do not recount,
After the long fatigue [of combat],
Before the tent of **Madawg** when they came back . . .

70A   MANUSCRIPT PAGE: 17.20–23, A TEXT

Early rising in the morning;
An estuary battle, before a border:
There was a breach, there was charging,
[There was] fire.
Like a boar you led [men] up the hill.
He was tenacious, he was courteous, was grave:
Hawks in dark armour were covered in blood.

70B   MANUSCRIPT PAGE: 36.12–15, B TEXT

An early rising in the morning
To do battle with a chief before the border.
There was bitter fighting[1]
In the front line of battle.
A very dear friend,
Where he pleases.[2]
He was tenacious, he was courteous, was grave:
He was a dark pillar of war.

71A   MANUSCRIPT PAGE: 18.1–6, A TEXT

An early rising in the morning,
From the darkening mouth of a river
In front of the border.
From front to front pursuing,
Leading a hundred, he charged first.
It was fiercely that you
Used to make the blood flow –
Like drinking mead while laughing.
Like a lion did you
Use to cause slaughter
With a thrusting fast and furious.
It was very eagerly that he,
Gwrhafal, used to kill the enemy
Wherever he would be.

---

1 R. cyfarth
2 R. yn yd gre

An early rising in the morning
When warriors in an army hurry forth.
From front to front pursuing,
Before a hundred he struck first,
He was as eager for slaughter
As [for] drinking wine or mead.
It was without pity
He'd kill the enemy,
Ithael, an eager attack[er].[1]

---

1 R. gorddin

[MANY OBSCURITIES]
He fell head first into the depths,
The skilful leader did not
Hold on to his intention;
His killing on a spear
Was a breach of privilege.
It was **Owain**'s custom
To climb onto the rampart
Couching his best spear
Before attacking, seeking slaughter:
A battle-lion lost.[1]
Fair, swift in giving, swift in battle,
He brought (feats of his gauntlet) pale death[2]
With his armour-stripping hand.
The chieftain gave me payment
With his costly spear-fighting.
Praise be to the sad, fierce [one]:
White are his cheeks.
He was modest when a maid
Was main arbiter;
He was a possessor
Of horses, and dark armour
And shields the colour of ice,
Side by side with comrades striking,
Retreating[3] and attacking.

---

1 R. cadlew
2 R. angau glas aswyddau loflen
3 Retreating: retreat may have been a part of the strategy of warfare.

A war leader, he led into battle.
The people of the land, they loved him,
The mighty reaper:
Green earth, [with] blood
On a new grave.
Over his red [garb]
He wore [his] armour.
A trampler on armour,
An armour trampler.
Like death, weariness descends:
Spears all shattered
At the beginning of battle;
The thrust of the spear
Was meant [in war] to clear the way.

I sang a famous song
Of the laying waste of your cell
And the hall that [once] used to be.
The storming with the dawn
Of the champion's dwelling –
That deserved mead, sweet, ensnaring:
A pretty gift to the hosts of the English!
Too great a penance is the time
They are allowed to live.
A liegeman of Gwynedd,
His glory shall be heard.
[His] grave is in Gwanannon.
The unyielding, the battle-mighty
Man of Gwynedd,
Bull of battle, violent
In the conflict of kings
Before the pressing of earth upon him,
Before [his] lying down.
The frontier region of Gododdin is his grave.

75A MANUSCRIPT PAGE: 19.4–10, A TEXT

An army well-accustomed to war;
A lord leading a host, cruel his hand.
He was wise and refined and proud,
Not ill-humoured in carousing.
Under his protection white horses moved;
It was not for the good of the land of Pobddelw!

[IW: From here on we have a fragment of another ode.]

We are called the wing and the front in combat,
In the breaking of spears, spears equal in rank.
The champion's skill with sharp iron
Provided protection in conflict,
A ploughshare in the din, in the uproar of battle;
He was a man with flaming steel,
Full of vigour against any foe.

75B MANUSCRIPT PAGE: 37.13–17, B TEXT

He encountered a harsh enemy,
The black killer of a plundering army.
He was not inconspicuous, was not fugitive,
At a feast he was not fugitive,
He was not bitter-sweet.
Under his protection white horses neighed –
It was not for the good of the land of Bod Erw!
The bull of battle did not retreat
The width of even one acre;
A man of dire purpose: **Llwyrddelw**.

[DISJOINTED]
He kept at Catraeth a herd
Of red war-steeds
And blood-stained war-armour.
In an army the spears in the front
Become wanton.[1]
The war-hound's wrath was [set]
Against a hill-fort.[2]
We're called the ones of bright,
[The ones] of brilliant fame.[3]
From the hand of **Heiddyn** [would come]
A shower of spears.

The courteous lord of Gododdin will be praised,
He was courteous in sharing, he will be lamented.
In front of Eidyn this spirit of flame will [never] return.
He set his chosen men in front,
He set a stout door against all attacks,
He set upon the fierce foe with spirit;
Because he feasted, he bore a great burden.
Of the men of Mynyddawg none escaped
Except one terrifying, weapon-brandishing [warrior].[4]

---

1 R. dyre
2 R. gwrth aerfre
3 R. ffofre
4 R. amddiffryd

Since the loss of **Morien** there's been no shield.
They supported, they praised the champion.[1]
He brought in his hand blue spears
(Heavy shafts put at risk this chief risk-taker)
On a dapple-grey and neck-arching horse.
The fallen in battle were [there],
Piled up in layers because of his blades.[2]
When he conquered in his fighting –
He was no deserter –
He deserved our praise
[And] mead, ensnaring and sweet.

---

1 R. traethiennyn
2 R. rac

I saw an array
That came from Kintyre,[2]
And gloriously did they
Attack around a raging fire.
I saw what was usual:
That they brought it [= fire][3]
Onto a town.
And the warriors of Nwythion – they had lost.
I saw warriors in ranks coming and shouting:
And the head and arm of Dyfnwal –
Crows were pecking at them.[4]

---

1 An ode from Strathclyde. This does not belong to the *Gododdin*.
2 As Kenneth Jackson points out, this is a verse of heroic elegy of the same type as the odes of the *Gododdin*. It is a poem from Strad Clud (Strathclyde) and it commemorates, with glee, the killing of Dyfnwal Frych (*Domhnall Brecc* in Old Irish; Speckled Dyfnwal), king of Dál Riada, by the Britons of Strathclyde at the Battle of Strathcarron, near Falkirk, in 642. The leader of the Britons was King Hoan (Owain) son of Beli son of Nwython (Old Irish *Nechtan*). Kintyre (Welsh *Pentir*, Irish *Ceann Tíre* both meaning 'headland') is the Scottish peninsula, which would have been in the kingdom of Dál Riada.
3 R. rhyddygyn
4 Lit. *chewing them*

I saw an array
That came from Kintyre,
And a fairer conflagration
Did they bring.
I saw two from their town
Who had quickly fallen.
It was by the word of Nwython
That they had been incensed.
I saw great, mighty warriors
Who came with the dawn;
And the head of Dyfnwal Frych –
Crows were pecking at it.[1]

---

1 Lit. *chewing it*

Gwelais i ddull o Bentir a ddoyn,
A berth am goelcerth a ddisgynnyn.
Gwelais i ddau og eu tre re rygwyddyn,
O air Nwython rygoddesyn.
Gwelais i wŷr dulliawr gan wawr a ddoyn;
A phen Dyfnwal Frych, brain a'i cnoyn.

I saw an array
That came from Kintyre,
And they attacked,
They raised a raging fire.
I saw two from their town
Quickly descending.
Their arising was
At the bidding of Nwython.
I saw men in array
With the dawn coming;
And the head of Dyfnwal Frych –
Crows were pecking at it.

Lucky, victorious, lively and fair,
Back-bone of any timid host,
With his blue blade repelling
The foe from over the sea;
Manly and mighty,
With a massive great hand,[1]
Stout-hearted, most wise –
They besiege him.
His instinct – it was to attack
In front of nine champions,
In the presence of army and troops
And provoke them.
I love the victor, there was a couch
Beneath him:[2]
Cynddilig of Aeron,[3] praiseworthy and bold.

----

1 R. law
2 R. adanaw
3 Aeron: see Ode 18.

I would have loved to attack
In the front, at Catraeth,
In payment for mead in the hall
And a draught of wine.
I would have loved him who did not[1]
Find any fault in a spear
Before he was killed,
Away from his green Uffin.[2]
I would have loved fame like him
Who caused the shedding of blood;
He brandished his sword with great wrath.[3]
A brave man does not tell,[4]
Before Gododdin,
That the **son of Ceidiaw** was not
Praised above all warriors.

---

1 R. ni
2 Uffin: probably the name of a place or territory.
3 R. yng ngoeithin
4 R. nis

After war it is woeful for me
To endure the agony
Of death through [great] suffering;
And a second heavy woe is it for me
To see the falling,
Head first, of our warriors.
[There's] dolour and long sighing
After the splendid warriors
Of our land and territory:
Rhufawn and **Gwgawn**,
Gwiawn and **Gwlged**,
Men of the bravest stations in battle,
Mighty men in conflict.
May there be for their souls, after battle,
A welcome in the land of Heaven,
The dwelling place of plenty.

He hurled back an attack
Above a pool of blood,
Like a brave man he struck
Any rank that did not retreat.
Tafloyw with a flourish would
Knock back a glass full of mead:
Before kings he would
Knock back an army.
His counsel was awaited
Where many dared not speak:
And had he been unpleasant
He would not have been heard.[1]
Before the onslaught of axe-blows
And sharpened swords
What is seen is what will
[Later] be read out aloud.

---

1 R. endewid

Haven of the army,
Spear of that haven
With an honoured company,
In a place of honour
On the day of battle.
In conflict
They were ruthless,
After drunkenness
And imbibing of mead.
From our victorious attacking
There was no escaping
On the day of mighty charging:[1]
By the time that this was told
A host of men and horses
Had been broken;
That was the fate of **Tyngyr.**

---

1 R. yn nydd

When many cares
Come upon me,
I consider my fear
With failing breath –
[As if in] lively running –
And straightaway I weep.
For a dear one I'd grieve,
A dear one I'd loved,
A stag of great renown.
Woe unto him who used to
Fall into rank
With the men of Argoed.[1]
It was well that he
Put pressure on an army –
For the good of kings –
Against rough wooden [shafts],
Against a flood of grief
In return for feasting.
In a circle round a feast
He led us [all]
Up to a glowing fire,
To a white skin
And to fresh drink.[2]
Geraint: before those from the South

---

1 Argoed: a place name of two elements: *ar* + *coed* = 'on/near a wood'. There
was an Argoed Llwyfain ('llwyfain' meaning elmwood) in the Old North; it is
mentioned in a poem by another *cynfardd*, Taliesin. There was also an Argoed
in Powys, in the north-east of Wales.
2 R. llyn gosgroyw

A battle-cry was raised,
Brilliant white [was] the bright shape[1]
On this lord's shield;
The spear of this generous lord [was] renowned.
Sea's bounty! I know his nature,[2]
I know **Geraint**: you were generous
[And] eminent.

86   MANUSCRIPT PAGE: 21.19–23, A TEXT

Unhampered his renown,
[Unhampered was] his eminence;
An immovable anchor in conflict;
Unyielding eagle of wrathful warriors;
Purposeful in battle, **Eiddef** was dazzling;
In battle he went out
In front of the very fast horses,
He had been brought up
On wine from a cup.
Before a green grave
And before his cheek grew pale
He was a man for a feast
Over excellent mead from a cup.

---

1 R. dull
2 R. gogwn i eisyllud

Deadly against every champion:
His drinking-horn[1]
Was filled as if to the brim;
The face of his shield was shattered;
Impetuous and savage [was he],
Defender of Rhufoniawg.[2]
In a second battle around the Aled
His war horses
And his blood-stained armour
Were called for.
Immovable in any army:
Where the mighty in battle may be
There will be a place
With blood-red pebbles when they,
[The warriors], are incensed to fury.
In battle, with a bitter blade,
With great force he smote;
He brought from combat
A warning: he would lay out
Pale corpses.[3]
Any lady, and maiden, and lord
Could approach **the son of Erfai,**
Could approach the arrogant boar;
And since he was
The son of a lawful king,

---

1 R. bual
2 Rhufoniawg / Rhufoniog is in north Wales. Aled is a river in Rhufoniog.
3 R. cann celain

Of the blood of the men of Gwynedd,
Of Clyd[1] Gwaredawg,[2]
Before the cheek of the generous one,
The wise one, the one unperturbed
Was buried in earth
[He was] one of high praise and of gift[s].[3]
There's a grave for **Garthwys Hir**,
[The one] from the land of Rhufoniawg.

---

1 Clyd may be a man's name.
2 Gwaredawg / Gwaredog is a place name in Gwynedd.
3 R. echiawg

Deadly against every champion:
His drinking-horn[1]
Was filled as if to the brim;
The face of his shield was shattered,
Impetuous and splendid [was he],
Defender of Rhufoniawg.
In a second battle around the Aled
His war horses
And his blood-stained armour
Were seen.
Let them be immovable,
Let their gift[s] be large,
Let them be of great fury
When they are incensed.
In battle, with a bitter blade,
With great force he smote,
He brought from combat
A warning;
At the Calends he provided song[s].
Any lady, and maiden, and lord
Could approach **the son of Erfai**,
Could approach the arrogant boar;
And since he was the son of a lawful king,
A lord of Gwynedd, of the blood
Of Cilydd[2] Gwaredawg,

---

1 R. bual
2 Where 87A has Clyd, 87B has Cilydd.

Before the cheek of the generous one,
The wise one, the prudent one
Was buried in earth
His gift and his fame were sought;
And it is sad that there's a grave[1]
For **Gorthyn Hir,**
[A man] from the high land of Rhufoniawg.

---

1 R. echiawg

Dinogad's[1] coat is one of many colours,
One of many colours –
I made it of the skins of martens.
Wheesht![2] Wheesht! A whistling!
I used to sing, the eight slaves sang
When your dad went out to hunt,
A spear on his shoulder, a club in his hand;
He'd call the dogs,
Each one as quick as the other,
"Giff, Gaff, catch catch, fetch fetch!"
In a coracle he would kill
A fish, as when a lion
Kills its prey.
When your dad went to the mountain
He'd bring back one roebuck,
One wild boar, one stag,

---

1 This verse has been called a lullaby. It may also be a hunting-song. The words
are those of a mother – presumably – who may have a small boy, Dinogad, on
her knee. She may well tuck at his coat while proclaiming or singing. When
she refers to the various animals his 'dad' caught she may have assumed the
numbering with fingers that is a feature of some children's verse.

It is strange to find a poem like this in the middle of savage war odes; but
the *Gododdin* was, presumably, the work of a *bardd teulu*, literally, a poet of
the *llu tŷ*, the retinue of the house, or court. In due course it became one of the
household poet's duties to sing to the lady of the court – in a quiet voice, so as
not to disturb the serious business of the men, who were probably thinking up
plans to raid and plunder. It may be that a household poet in the Old North
composed it.

To assume, as some have done, that the author of this poem may be a woman
is as unlikely as that Lady Macbeth composed her own lines.

2 'Wheesht' is an attempt to convey the whistling sound in the original.

One speckled grouse from the mountain,
One fish from the Falls of Derwennydd.[1]
Of all that your dad could reach with his flesh-hook
Of wild boar and foxes
And creatures in bushes,
Not one would escape
Unless very well-winged.[2]

---

1 Derwennydd is a waterfall on one of the Derwent rivers in the north of England. R. Geraint Gruffydd has suggested that these are the Lodore Falls on Watendlath Beck, above Derwentwater, which would have been in the old British kingdom of Rheged. He dates the poem c.650.
2 The final lines are very much like an old farmer's traditional saying in Anglesey about the quality of his hedge: "'Daiff dim drwyddo, ond a hedo" (Nothing will get through it, unless it can fly).

Distress, unsought, assailed me;
There comes not, there will not
Come over me
Anything that can be more heavy.
There's no one reared in a hall
Who is more brave than he,
Nor any man who is
In battle more steadfast;
And on Rhyd Benclwyd[1] his horses were in front,
His fame – it was far-reaching;
His chalked [shield] – it was shattered;
And before **Gwair Hir** was laid in the earth
He deserved his mead-horns, this **only son of Fferfarch**.

Three hundred warriors, gold-torqued,
They attacked, defending their land:
There was slaughter.
[But] though they were killed, they [also] killed.
And till the end of the world they will be
Held in great glory.
And of those of us, kinsmen, who went –
Alas! – except for one man, no one escaped.

---

1 The location of Rhyd Benclwyd (or the Ford of Penclwyd) is not known.

Three hundred gold-torqued,
Of great prowess, aggressive;[1]
Three hundred haughty [warriors]
Of one mind and fully armed;
Three hundred fierce horses
Charged with them;
Three hounds[2] and three hundred –
Alas! – they didn't return.

Savage in battle, mighty in combat;
In conflict he'd not make any truce,
In the day of wrath he'd not evade a fight;
Bleiddig son of Eli was a boar for fury.
He had drunk wine from full vessels of glass;
And on the day of battle
He'd perform great feats
From the back of a white steed.
Before he died[3]
He left corpses behind him,[4]
[All] coloured red.

---

1 R. gwaenawg
2 Three hounds = warriors; heroes, and three hundred. Does this mean 300 warriors and their 3 leaders, each of the 3 being a centurion?
3 R. no'i
4 R. edewai

93   MANUSCRIPT PAGE: 32.16-21, B TEXT

A shield withstanding attack,
He'd not submit to any one;
A love of honour – he would nurture that.
Unheeding, he, of armour,[1]
[With] horses on the battle-front.
In battle they sowed spears
Of holly stained with blood.
When my friend was struck, he struck others,
There was no insult he would bear.
Faithful in guarding the ford,
He loved it when he carried off
The champion's portion in the hall.[2]

94   MANUSCRIPT PAGE: 33.4–9, B TEXT

Heaven's protection,
A dwelling in a yearned-for land!
Woe to us because of sorrow
And [this] unceasing sadness.
When noble men came from
The region of Din Eidyn,
The chosen men of all enlightened lands,
To do battle with the mongrel men of Lloegr,
There were nine score against each one,[3]
[Nine score] about each mail-clad man,
A multitude of horses, silk clothes and armour:
Gwaednerth in battle defended his honour.

---

1 R. seirch
2 R. cyfran
3 For the literal-minded: if there were nine score, that is 180 men against every one of Mynyddawg's men, of which there were 300, the Anglian army was 54,000 strong.

The host of Gododdin on horses,
Rough-maned, of the colour of swans,
In full-combat harness,
And in the army's front line
Attacking in a crowd,
Defending the woods
And [defending] the mead of Eidyn.
By the counsel of Mynyddawg
Shields had been shattered,[1]
And blades had fallen
Upon white cheeks.
They loved to attack with long spears:[2]
They bore no shame, those men who did not flee.

I, reared on wine, drank mead
In one draught on my way
In front of Catraeth.
When he, the steadfast in battle,
Struck with his blades –
Where he was to be seen
He wasn't feeble!
In liberation he, the deadly shield-bearer[3]
Madawg of Elfed,[4] was no unsightly spectre.[5]

---

1 R. torasai
2 R. gan gwial laes
3 R. sgwydog
4 Elfed (Elmet), a British kingdom, situated around the the modern city of Leeds.
5 R. edellyll

97   MANUSCRIPT PAGE: 34.4–6, B TEXT

When he came to battle, he[1]
Was not one to flee
For his life.
The avenger of Arfon,[2]
Defender of Britons[3]
Went to war for gold decorations:[4]
The horses of **Cynon** were frisky.

98   MANUSCRIPT PAGES: 34.16–35.3, B TEXT

There will come to me today[5] –
From the hand of **Heinif**,[6] –
The wealth of Unhwch,[7]
[He] of the best of families.
He killed a great host
To gain reputation.
The **son of Nwython** killed –
Of gold-torqued warriors –
A hundred princes
So he might be praised.
It was even better when he went
With warriors to Catraeth.

---

1 R. i gyfranc
2 Arfon was in Gwynedd, in north Wales.
3 R. arwrthiad
4 R. ceinion
5 R. gwowy; heddiw
6 R. heinim = heinif. The name of the hero is Heinif, and *heinif* means *lively* or *agile*.
7 R. anlloedd

He was well nurtured, was reared on wine,[1]
[He was] great of heart;
He was a grey man [but] was *agile*,
He was a scatterer of mail-coats,
He was fierce, he was savage
On the back of his horse.
There was no man who wore
Armour for battle,[2]
No man who was [more] *lively*
With spear and shield
And his sword and his knife,[3]
[No man] who was better than
Heinif son of Nwython.[4]

*99 MANUSCRIPT PAGE: 35.4–5, B TEXT[5]

From over the Sea of Iuddew,[6] in battle most valiant;
Three times more fierce than any fierce lion,
Bubon acted with great fury.[7]

---

1 R. aillt
2 R. ymlhymlwyd
3 R. a'i . . . a'i
4 R. heinim
5 This type of verse is an *englyn*, which became one of the 24 strict metres of the professional poets.
6 The Sea of Iuddew is the Firth of Forth.
7 R. bar dew

It was usual [for him], on a lively horse,[1]
To defend Gododdin
In the front line of the battle of the fierce men;
It was usual for him
To be quick on the track of a deer;
It was usual for him
To attack in the face
Of the household guard of Deira;
It was usual for **the son of Golystan**
(Though his father was no king)
To be listened to when he spoke.
It was usual, for the good of Mynyddawg,
To have shattered shields and a red spear
Before a lord of Eidyn Urfai.[2]

---

1 R. DH: gnaut = gnawd
2 Part of the last line can be translated as 'the lord of Eidyn, Urfai'. So why bother with Mynyddawg as the lord of Eidyn? It is highly unlikely that a man whose father was no king would be the lord of Eidyn. Ifor Williams suggested that 'Eidyn Urfai' might be the full name of 'Eidyn'.

His blades were seen in the warband
Withstanding the hard foe.
There was a retreat
Before the clanking of his shield:
In front of the rock of Eidyn
A multitude fled.[1]
Whatever his hand seized[2]
He'd not return it;
There was wax upon it,
And there was fire from it,[3]
[From] the battered shield of the resolute one;
When he thrust, he [really] thrust[4] –
He did not thrust a second time;
What he cut through was really gutted.
Frequent, after a feast,
Was his 'gift'[5] to the enemy –
He was treated bitterly![6]
And before he was buried
Under a covering of earth
Edar deserved his draught of mead.

---

1 R. efrifed
2 R. gaffai ei law
3 R. ac thaned
4 R. grynied
5 The reference to a 'gift' is ironic; the next statement tells what really happened.
6 R. yd draethed

He attacked in front of three hundred of the best,
He smote in the middle and [killed in] the wing;
He was splendid in front of the noblest of hosts,
He gave gifts of horses from the herd in winter,
On the rampart of a fort, he fed black crows –
Although he was not Arthur.[1]
Among the mighty in conflict,[2]
In the front line he,
Gwawrddur, was an alder tree.

---

1 The reference to Arthur may be the very first reference to one who later became the legendary King Arthur. The alder tree is, like a 'pillar' or a 'post', a metaphor for the immovable hero.
2 R. rhwng cyfnerthi yng nghlysur

He fed birds with his hand,[1]
I admire him, who caused terror,[2]
The destroyer, [and the] ravager.[3]
He wore gold
In the front line of battle,
In the terrible conflict of warriors.
The freckled war-sustainer,
One of the Violent Three,[4]
Pursuer in combat,
A fearsome bear, an attacker,[5]
A retinue's inciter,
The toast of a vast host,
He, **Cibno, son of Gwengad**,
Was handsome.[6]

---

1 R. a'i adaf
2 R. add-ofn-iad
3 R. eithiniad
4 A reference to a Triad about Violent Men.
5 R. arwygiad
6 R. cain

The Gorchanau[1]

✳ GORCHAN TUDFWLCH
The Song / Incantation of Tudfwlch

MANUSCRIPT PAGES: 25.1–26.7, A TEXT

Weapons scattered,
Ranks [all] broken,
The tumult of slaughter:
[This] in the presence of affluence,
In the presence of magnificence,
In the presence of splendour.
A bitter cup of alder [wood],
And drinking horns all bent,
And sword[s] bent too.

To praise a champion
Of kingly hosts in front!
[He is now] the colour of ashes.
Where I saw [him]
Grass sprouted forth,

---

1 I have divided the lines in the way that makes the best sense to me. For another division of lines, for a different purpose from mine, see Kathryn A. Klar in *Early Welsh Poetry*, edited by Brynley F. Roberts.

From the fetter of oppression.
Unparallelled hero,
Praised lord, powerful and gentle.
And Rhuddforfa[1]
And Morfa
And Eifionydd[2]
Lamented the day of splendid pomp,
[The day of] plentiful trivets
[Provided] according to his custom –
As [at] Tal Rhosedd.[3]
The loud thunder [of lament]
Around Tal Henban[4] was excessive.
A wolf in his life:
He was like a wolf at the ford in his prime;
His eyes [were] beams,
Shining serpent-like
From a serpent's nest.[5]
Mighty are you,
Snare of oppressors, beloved of girls;
You loved to live
Dangerously:
I loved you alive.
Rampart of valour,
Heroic bull,

---

1 'Rhuddforfa' (literally, red seashore): there is a Morfa Coch by Dinas Dinlle, near Caernarfon.

2 Eifionydd is a region in Gwynedd. As it is regions in north Wales that seem to lament his death, it may be that Tudfwlch came from this part of Wales.

3 Tal Rhosedd: was it a court famed for its generosity?

4 Tal Henban: there is a Talhenbont and a Henbant Mawr in Eifionydd.

5 llwch nadredd: *a plant*?

I lament your death; you loved war –
[You] of the fury of the sea –
In the front line of warriors[1]
About Catpwll,[2]
A Brân[3] of wide praise
Fighting in Cynwyd.[4]
A wave arose from Cyfryngon,[5]
World's splendour;
He drove back
On the path of the land –
For the good of the foot soldiers –
Four hosts,
Four armies of the world
With round shield[s] in tatters,
With blade in hair,
[With] spears, four-sided, in four directions:
A warrior without any restraint!

From blue horns, in the morning, mead;
A warrior of rightful titles
From among those [wearing] purple,
A haven for an army.
Tudfwlch's arm . . .

[TWO LINES LOST . . . ? *brandished weapons?*]
. . . With terrible fury,
Head of the blood of the host.

---

1 R. gwyr gwnedd
2 R. cad + pwll. Catpwll: a place name.
3 R. Brân clod lydan. Brân: there are many heroes called Brân. Tudfwlch fought
like one of them.
4 Cynwyd: a place not far from Corwen.
5 Cyfryngon: an unknown place. If this is a jumbled up *Caer Wyragon* (> Caer-
wrangon), then that would be Worcester.

For mead and beer
They went, a crowd, over their border
To the station of spears in battle.
To preserve what was right, they were bold –
Cynan and Cynon,
Teithfyw of Mona,[1] by the right of his lineage;
Tudfwlch and Cyfwlch
Made a breach on the top of the strongholds.
With Mynyddawg,[2]
Their drinks were bitter:
For me [there will be] a year of longing
For the men of Catraeth, who reared me,
For their steel blades,
For their pure mead from drinking horns.[3]
Weapons scattered,
Ranks [all] broken, I heard the tumult [of it].

And that is how it ends.
Now begins the Song of Adebon.

---

1 Mona is Anglesey.
2 Mynyddawg is mentioned. The warriors are called 'the men of Catraeth'. The 'me' in 'who reared me' is, presumably, meant to be Aneirin.
3 R. bualau

✳ GORCHAN ADEBON[1]
The Song / Incantation of Adebon

MANUSCRIPT PAGE: 26.8–16, A TEXT

An apple from an apple-tree will not fall for long.
The wicked and the furious – they won't prosper.
The naked is not fearless, in the midst of nettles!
When their fates decree it, all men die.
The one I loved – he loved booty.
No man dies twice.
The utterance of the man who is mute
Lacks any shape.
A fellow-countryman does not like to cause fear.
The horses of a fiery youth are very white.
There's great contention for the horn of Cuhelyn.
In habitation, peace was lost.
[The man] with wide scar[s], you were
Bold on the day of battle.
Seekers seek a hidden world.[2]
That slender lad with his head held high
Is reaper of his enemies.
Your mark of approval on the Song of Adebon.

That is how the Song of Adebon ends.
Here now begins the Song of Cynfelyn.

---

1 This *gorchan* is an assortment of proverbs and gnomic observations.
2 R. cuddfyd

* GORCHAN CYNFELYN
The Song / Incantation of Cynfelyn

MANUSCRIPT PAGES: 26.18–28.6, A TEXT

If I were to compose it,
If I were to sing it
The mountain tops would [all] resound.[1]

The spear, the torque of Twrch Trwyth[2] –
Foul of crotch, [and] notably terrible:
He made for a river
Before his precious possessions [were all snatched].
The horses trampled up the mound.
Before the hoofs of the grunter
[There were] veteran warriors,
Mighty-boned horsemen.
He dug up a breach:
The courage of the destroyer!
The Ford of Gwyn . . .

Face to face with Angles it is right to kill.[3]
Rightly did they, in battle, cause damage
Before a [steed], thoroughbred and white:
It was with audacity that Dywel
Was well able to attack –

---

1 R. tardei gorchegin
2 The warriors of Cynfelyn are compared with the warriors of King Arthur. This section refers to an episode in the story of *Culhwch and Olwen* where Arthur's knights try to snatch a pair of scissors, a comb and a razor from between the ears of the savage boar called Twrch Trwyth.
3 The next section is one about the prowess of Cynfelyn and his warriors.

For every man of Deira your blow [struck]
Through stud, through rivet,
Through cover-skin and leather
And [a shield's] gold cover.
And deep distress will come
To Gwynasedd Felyn[1] –
His blood [will be] about him;
The foaming head of mead,
Fine and yellow, will be hidden.
His blood [will be] about him[2]
In front of the hosts of Cynfelyn,
Cynfelyn the wrathful,
Bold, with his spear foremost,
One who feeds birds
On corpses [all] covered in blood.
Long-stepping steeds galloped
Beneath the thighs of chieftains,
As swift in motion as wild men
Over fields of grass.
A lord, a gift to his land:
It is my lot to lament him
Till I may reach my day of silence.
Hewer of the enemy
With [a] weapon, massive-hafted.

---

1 Gwynasedd Felyn: probably a place name. But it could refer to a Gwynasedd
(wife of) Belyn.
2 R. ei

The Song of Cynfelyn[1]
Is the pride of honourable hosts.
The Song of Cynfelyn, the guardian of the borderland;
A discerning warrior, Gwynedd was his land,
?Valiant attackers praise [him].

The fort of Eidyn, thrusters bright [and] young,
Fair grassland – red;
Horses worth the payment of exalted mead,[2]
The horses of Eithinyn:
They are splendid.

The Song of Cynfelyn
Attached to *Gododdin*
Has made full mention of the man.

He gave me his spear, all gilded with gold:
May it be for the good of his soul.
Tegfan's son is admired
For the number and the giving [of gifts],
The grandson of Cadfan, pillar of battle.
When weapons were hurled
Over the heads of the wolves of war
The two were quick in the day of conflict.

---

1 I have, like a clueless scribe, set out these lines – and those below – to the right, and have treated them as verse. They are probably some other poor, puzzled, clueless scribe's or scribes' attempt or attempts to explain to himself / themselves what this poem means.
2 R. emys

Three men and three score and three hundred
Went to the land of Catraeth:
Of those who rushed forth
After mead [served up] by servants
Except for three,
None [of them] came back –
Cynon and Cadraith, and Cadlew from Cadnant;[1]
And I from my blood-letting.[2]
The true son of prophecy, they made up my ransom
With pure gold and silver and steel;
It was hurt, [and] not favour they got.

> This is the Song of the hosts of Cynfelyn
> Who stained [many men] with blood.

Here ends the Song of Cynfelyn.

---

1 Cadnant: a common place name.
2 Is the first person in this line 'Aneirin'? Does this section belong to a tale about Aneirin?

Every awdl *[ode] of the Gododdin is worth one song in singing because of [its] honour in a song competition [or bardic contest]. Every one of the Gwarchanau [Songs] is worth three songs and three score and three hundred. And the reason is for keeping memory in the Songs of the number of men who went to Catraeth. Than that a man ought to go to fight without arms, a poet ought not to go to a contention [bardic competition] without this Song.*

Here now begins the Song of Maeldderw. Taliesin sang it and gave honour to it. [It is worth] as much as all the awdlau *[odes] of the Gododdin and its three Songs[1] in a song competition.*

---

1 The Three Songs would presumably be the Songs of Tudfwlch, Adebon, and Cynfelyn.

* GORCHAN MAELDDERW[1]
The Song / Incantation of Maeldderw[2]

MANUSCRIPT PAGES: 28.18–30.11, A TEXT

About a fort are two loops of estuaries.
I'm woken up, in a whitewashed [and] very bright [fort],
[By] the flashing and dashing, the harsh [man] of two battles,
Renowned one [and] seeker of war[s],
In textured plaid all stained with blood,
One invincible his charge since he was a youth,
He caused a breach, he did not retreat.

Of Aeneas' creed [was he], of gentle nature;[3]
[Yet] in arms he scowled; [and] brisk,
[And] rash [was he] when called within the walls;
A warrior who, when called, would hurry.
In beer-hall, a humble [and] handsome bed-fellow
With no sign of sadness nor any trace [of it];[4]
In war, you were ferocious and audacious:
A frontier was breached, one of good entitlement.
Without measure was his fame,
[Though] for his greatness he wasn't too fussed.
A well-known secret . . .
He looked for victory, [rather than] a maid –
A shining one, an importuner, dignified of brow,[5]

---

1 This poem is, supposedly, the work of Taliesin.
2 In this *gorchan*, as in the *gorchan* of Adebon, there are proverbs, wise sayings, and gnomic statements. This material is mixed with many lines of heroic verse.
3 R. adef
4 R. edrywyn
5 R. adon

On a red dragon, a Pharaoh's prize:[1]
Friendly in the breeze – Addaon.
He who fell [in battle], died, and his whelp[2]
By torture with strong steel;
Running man and footman gone,[3]
His retinue –
A wall of ashen spears on a sea!

Neither *enemy attack* [?] nor counsel
Would hold the borders, soul unyielding.
It would not be of greater use his
Rushing forth, rushing forth –
The outer door of Eidyn fort.

Fair Cynan,[4] a front-line rampart of an army,
He struck his sword
On the dyke of cowards.
Victorious his lord, bold,[5]
One of strong protection, a lord
Whose ferocity was [great],
He was one of the main men of Cynlas,[6]
Of a world that's deeply founded.

Too sweet, [and] it is vomited:[7]
He desired the very bitter.[8]

---

1 Does this refer to a horse?
2 R. geneu
3 R. tuth a phedyt; myned
4 Cynan: may well be the name of a hero.
5 R. ener en hy
6 Cynlas: a king called Cynlas was scourged by the monk Gildas in the sixth
century, but this may be a place name.
7 R. rychwech; ry
8 R. rychwerw rychwenyches

May he desire the shelter of Enlli.[1]
He who took [the champion's] portion,[2]
The lucky portion was, in the morning,
On the border, [its] defence.
He seduced, he plays with the proud,[3]
Finds a place for the proudest men.
After plenty, [all] was lost:[4]
Drunkenness, lost; delight was lost.[5]

Rhun[6] of the North, [a] lord defends [him].

The very fat, his shape's[7] too big,
[And] bigger grows.
It's not only the honeysuckle[8]
That they call 'a wood'.
Fury's woven very easily, very quickly:
Fury's woven by slander into spears.
Vexed is the front [line of battle]; bent the tops of trees.
A lord, he has three-legged [cauldrons].
The red-eyed one, he sees [things] red.[9]
The world has not enough to satisfy ambition.[10]
Faultless fury is [like] the ploughing of the sea.
The first horse to act is the pale-white horse.

---

1 Enlli: this is the island of Bardsey, off the Llŷn peninsula. R. rychwenychwy;
gwales
2 R. a lewis
3 R. hutei
4 R. rhywdd
5 R. meddwyd
6 Rhun: probably a man.
7 R. dichwel. This section is one of gnomic wisdom and nature descriptions.
8 R. melfid
9 R. i rudd drem, drem rudd
10 R. digon. This line is duplicated.

Llwyrddelw's[1] throne is [full of] fury:
Before his burial he was a strong pillar.
A great man's gift to [all] poor men – Maeldderw![2]
The creator, the most bountiful [man in] his land.[3]
A spear's a warrant for the glory of a high ruler.
The land that desires – its desire will come to it.
A champion attacking, equally good in defending.[4]
His running was [such] as if a fiend[5]
Was in pursuit of him.
At last he won his way to Heaven.[6]
Shame won't win the smallest thing.

---

1 Llwyrddelw: an unknown man.
2 Maeldderw: another unknown man.
3 R. dieirydaf; erw
4 R. cy-mre
5 R. rhag
6 R. godiwedd

A Select Bibliography

Marged Haycock: *Legendary Poems from the Book of Taliesin* (2007, CMCS Publications)

Daniel Huws (ed.), *Llyfr Aneirin, a Facsimile* (1989, South Glamorgan County Council; National Library of Wales)

Ifor Williams (ed.), *Canu Aneirin* (1938, University of Wales Press)

Ifor Williams (ed.), *Canu Llywarch Hen* (1953, University of Wales Press)

Ifor Williams (ed.), *Canu Taliesin* (1960, University of Wales Press)

J. E. Caerwyn Williams, *The Poems of Taliesin,* An English version with additional material of *Canu Taliesin* (1968, The Dublin Institute for Advanced Studies)

TRANSLATIONS

Kenneth H. Jackson (ed.), *The Gododdin: The Oldest Scottish Poem* (1969, Edinburgh University Press)

A. O. H. Jarman (ed.), *Aneirin: Y Gododdin, Britain's Oldest Heroic Poem* (1988, Gomer Press)

John T. Koch (ed.), *The Gododdin of Aneirin* (1997, University of Wales Press)

These three books provide a full bibliography of relevant literature.

SEE ALSO

Joseph P. Clancy, *The Earliest Welsh Poetry* (1970, Macmillan)

Anthony Conran, *The Penguin Book of Welsh Verse* (1967, Penguin Books), subsequently published as, *Welsh Verse* (1992, Seren)

There are other, earlier translations, which have not been listed here, and translations in books on Celtic poets and the Celtic heroic age.

The most accessible discussions on the Book of Aneirin may be found in:

Rachel Bromwich & R. Brinley Jones (eds.), *Astudiaethau ar yr Hengerdd – Studies in Old Welsh Poetry* (1978, University of Wales Press)

Brynley F. Roberts (ed.), *Early Welsh Poetry* (1988, National Library of Wales)

Huw Pryce (ed.), *Literacy in Medieval Celtic Societies* (1998, Cambridge University Press), discusses orality and literacy.

Rachel Bromwich, *Trioedd Ynys Prydein – The Welsh Triads* (1961, University of Wales Press). This is the book to consult about Welsh lore.

About the Author

Professor Gwyn Thomas is a Welsh poet, academic and a former National Poet of Wales. Raised in Tanygrisiau and Blaenau Ffestiniog, he was educated at Ysgol Sir Ffestiniog, Bangor University and Jesus College, Oxford. Professor Thomas is presently Emeritus Professor of Welsh at Bangor University, Gwynedd. Gwyn Thomas has published 19 volumes of poetry, several volumes of work as a literary and cultural critic and commentator, volumes of adaptations and translations of medieval Welsh tales, and *Dafydd ap Gwilym: his Poems*, a translation of the complete work of the fourteenth-century Welsh poet.